Slinging the Bull in Korea

Slinging the Bull in Korea

An Adventure in Psychological Warfare

John Martin Campbell

With an introduction by Katherine Kallestad

John Martin Campbell

*For Hal Conklin, the Bard
of New Haven, and a bright
Star in the profession of
anthropology from Jack Campbell*

UNIVERSITY OF NEW MEXICO PRESS

Albuquerque

Text © 2010 by John Martin Campbell
Introduction © 2010 by Katherine Kallestad

All rights reserved. Published 2010
Printed in the United States of America
15   14   13   12   11   10   1   2   3   4   5   6

Library of Congress Cataloging-in-Publication Data

Campbell, John Martin, 1927–

Slinging the bull in Korea : an adventure in psychological warfare /
John Martin Campbell; with an introduction by Katherine Kallestad.
    p. cm.
Includes bibliographical references and index.

ISBN 978-0-8263-4876-0 (cloth : alk. paper)

1. Campbell, John Martin, 1927–
2. Korean War, 1950–1953—Personal narratives, American.
3. Korean War, 1950–1953—Psychological aspects.
4. Psychological warfare—Korea.
5. United States. Air Force—Biography.
6. Soldiers—United States—Biography.
 I. Kallestad, Katherine.
 II. Title.

DS921.6.C298 2010
951.904'28—dc22
[B]   2009034409

For Susan

Contents

Preface.. ix

Acknowledgments.. xi

Map of Korea, Spring 1950 xiv

Introduction by Katherine Kallestad............................. 1

Chapter One: Active Duty..................................... 23

Chapter Two: Mountain Home and Georgetown........................ 39

Chapter Three: The Voice of America and Clark Field................ 55

Chapter Four: Korea 76

Chapter Five: The Leaflet Campaign............................ 97

Notes... 165

Bibliography... 169

Index... 173

Preface

The title of this book is derived from a sign that in the fall of 1951 was posted beside a U.S. Air Force squadron headquarters at Gowan Field on the outskirts of Boise, Idaho. It contained a painting of the head of a snorting bull under which in bold script was written EL TORO ES MAS FUERTE QUE LA BALA, "The Bull Is Mightier Than the Bullet." The sign testified to the recent creation of an air force enterprise in psychological warfare, an enterprise prompted by confusion and fear among the Western Allies as they stood witness to increasing Soviet expansionism in Europe and the Far East, and prompted most particularly by the North Korean invasion of South Korea on the 25th of June 1950. As the military historian Michael Haas (1997, 77) has remarked, the North Korean attack "rocked the United Nations like an earthquake." An earthquake indeed, whose history and consequences are explained by Katherine Kallestad in her introduction to this book.

The new air force psychological warfare effort, which went by the cover name of Air Resupply and Communications Service (ARCS), embraced a wide range of secretive operations, one of which called for the participation of patriotic junior officers who would practice the trade implied by the logo at Gowan Field. Among ARCS' diverse missions, most of which were hazardous, we recent college graduates were assigned to the relatively tame and unheroic duty of composing and delivering military propaganda. Our participation in this esoteric line of work spanned more than two years of adventure in such odd places, among others, as the Idaho desert, the canyons of Manhattan, and the hills of Korea, an adventure in applied psychology that is narrated in the following chapters.

With Kallestad's introduction as its base, the principal purpose of this book is that of providing a chronological account of training and operational duties in the elusive Air Resupply and Communications Service as they were experienced by a fledgling psywar officer whose primary assignments were in "leaflets." This narrative is accompanied by descriptions of ARCS' structure and purposes, and it includes as part of the adventure how this writer came to be an air force lieutenant, how we citizens of the Pacific Northwest reacted to the outbreak of the Korean War, and my impressions of the natural and social environments in which I traveled while on active duty.

Hopefully, these observations and opinions will prove useful additions to the excellent but small body of literature on an obscure dimension of what is commonly known as "The Forgotten War."

Acknowledgments

When in 2003 I got the idea of writing a personal history of the ARCS enterprise, I did not foresee what that venture would require in the way of academic labor. Early on I found that for essential background and explanatory data the book would demand extraordinary library and archival study as well as extensive interviews with appropriate civilian and military informants. Because at the time I was involved in another book, I called for help from Katherine Kallestad and Marjorie Kilberg Shea.

These two colleagues have been my principal literary critics and associates for the past twelve years. Katherine, an authoritative student of the practice of psychological warfare during the cold war, most particularly its use by the UN Command and the North Korean and Chinese forces during the Korean War, has written the introduction. Marjorie is a natural-born archival sleuth who has ferreted out much of the more arcane data contained in the following chapters. Both have provided me with a wealth of detail necessary to the aims of the narrative, and have contributed, in draft, passages in chapters 1, 3, and 5. And then Jennifer J. George, my much beloved friend and adviser, has tuned my prose. Suffice it to say that their work has been of first, crucial importance to the production of this book.

Among the most notable contributors, Colonel Michael E. Haas, U.S. Air Force, Retired, a combat veteran of more recent wars and a distinguished historian of U.S. military history in special operations and psychological warfare (see the bibliography), gave friendly, if critical, encouragement to the work in progress.

Military and civilian informants who provided us with essential data include Lieutenant Colonel William M. Samuels, U.S. Air Force (USAF), Retired, who when we were second lieutenants served with me in the country north of Seoul. Recent communications with former ARCS officers John R. Allen, Angelo J. Hillas, Frederic S. Brody, and Charles S. Grill have enhanced the extensive notes provided by Bill Samuels. Former Sergeant Paul A. Wolfgeher, U.S. Army, who served with the First Loudspeaker and Leaflet Company in Seoul, Korea, from 1952 through 1954, contributed a wealth of background information on the production and distribution of leaflets as well as his personal experiences during the leaflet campaign.

Master Sergeant Yancy D. Mailes, assisted by Master Sergeant Clifford Sibley, historians at Mountain Home Air Force Base, Mountain Home, Idaho, and Herbert A. Mason Jr., Command Historian, Air Force Special Operations, Hurlburt Field, Florida, were our chief sources of unpublished archival evidence relative to the founding and early development of ARCS. Professional historians and archivists Carl H. Bernhardt, Air Resupply and Communications Association, Cheshire, Connecticut; Heather C. Bourke and Lynn Conway, Georgetown University, Washington, DC; Michael Gray, The Voice of America, Washington, DC; James Howard, Maxwell Air Force Base, Montgomery, Alabama; and Jean Offut, U.S. Army, Fort Bliss, El Paso, Texas, contributed additional essential data.

As in times past, Dr. Patricia Nietfeld has been my expert consultant on style. I am indebted further to Lieutenant Colonel Kenneth A. Benson, U.S. Air Force, Retired, for his descriptions of air force structure and operations, and to Professor Harold C. Conklin, Yale University, for his comments on the military history of the Philippines.

Then I acknowledge with gratitude the following relatives, friends, and acquaintances who have contributed useful detail ranging from the effective range of a 155mm howitzer to the 1951 population of Boise, Idaho.

Thomas A. Adams, Master Sergeant, U.S. Air Force, Retired; Richard G. Allee, Captain, U.S. Merchant Marine; Rolene Barnett; Joseph Bermudez Jr.; Jane Campbell; Ernesto A. C de Baca, Airman Second Class, U.S. Air Force, Retired; Mark R. C de Baca, Petty Officer Third Class, U.S. Navy, Retired; Harry D. Cowell; Lorna C. Dempsey; Dr. Robert H. Dempsey; Emily Dewey; Ethelinda L. Dietz; Michael D. Dugre, Senior Master Sergeant, U.S. Air Force; Professor John Thomas Grissom; Mary Beth Hermans; Grace Hsu; Dieter Jester, First Sergeant, U.S. Army; Lawrence Jones; Bruce Kallestad; Robert G. Lalicker, Captain, U.S. Navy, Retired; Rebecca Lange, Captain, U.S. Air Force; Richard E. Leonard, Colonel, U.S. Army, Retired; Robert J. Mamuzich; Richard S. Martinez; Lloyd W. Mason Jr., Captain, U.S. Air Force, Retired; John M. McDowell, First Sergeant, U.S. Army, Retired; Professor Susan V. Richards; Professor Thomas E. Roll; James L. Sands, Master Sergeant, U.S. Army, Retired; Professor James M. Sebring; Lisa P. Smith; Professor Warren S. Smith; Debra Lynn Shoemaker;

Charles H. Spenser, Lieutenant, U.S. Navy; Robert F. Sullivan, Major, U.S. Air Force, Retired; and Margaret A. Weinrod. To all these generous contributors of their time and knowledge and to my editor Clark Whitehorn, copy editor Jill Root, and book designer Cheryl Carrington I offer many thanks and all best wishes.

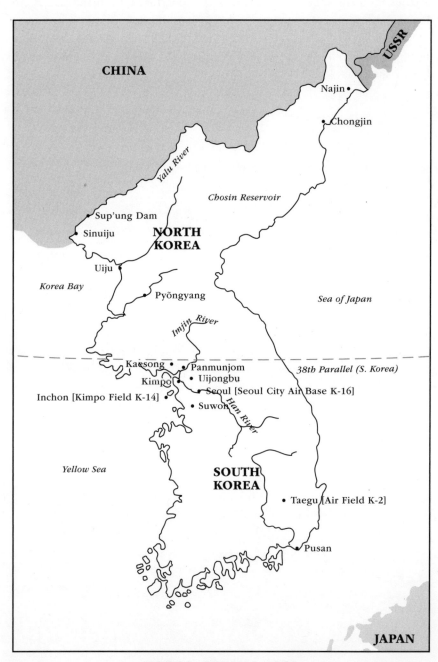

CHINA

USSR

Najin •

• Chongjin

Yalu River

Chosin Reservoir

• Sup'ung Dam

• Sinuiju

NORTH KOREA

Uiju •

Korea Bay

• Pyŏngyang

Sea of Japan

Imjin River

– – – Kaesong • • Panmunjom

Kimpo • • Uijongbu

38th Parallel (S. Korea)

Inchon [Kimpo Field K-14] • • Seoul [Seoul City Air Base K-16]

• Suwon

Han River

Yellow Sea

SOUTH KOREA

• Taegu [Air Field K-2]

• Pusan

JAPAN

KOREA, SPRING 1950

Introduction

Katherine Kallestad

The battles that raged the length and breadth of the rugged Korean peninsula from June 25, 1950, through July 27, 1953, cost in excess of four million lives, over half of them civilian.[1] In the summer of 2003, fifty years after the uneasy armistice, a reported 37,000 American troops still patrolled the 151-mile boundary between North and South Korea, roughly one soldier for every U.S. combat death of the Korean War (Brady 2003).

In the following chapters Jack Campbell takes us on a personal tour of his experiences as a psychological warfare officer in the Air Force 581st Air Resupply and Communications Service (ARCS) Wing during the Korean War. Born of cold war policies and politics and coming of age in the hot war strategies and tactics of Korea, the 581st ARCS illustrates the problems and promise of military units specifically designed to carry out both psychological warfare and special operations. Enjoying the advantage of thorough historical research by both civilian and military authors, veterans' recollections, and the release of recently declassified information, this introduction examines the causes and conduct of the Korean War and the concomitant evolution and growth of U.S. State and military organizations specializing in gathering, shaping, and acting on information vital to national security.

The need of democracies such as the United States to handle their own domestic politics, as well as to continue balancing forces globally against growing pressure exerted by established and emerging Communist nations such as the Soviet Union and China, had as much to do with the conduct and outcome of the Korean War as the deployment of armies or the use of military hardware. The Korean conflict that flared up just five years after the global firestorm of World War II was to be the first in a succession of limited, largely unwinnable wars. In these wars, fought not only in the fog of battle but in the mire of ideological rhetoric, victory would often become a matter of perception, a small balancing act on the brink of total destruction, in which carefully chosen words, whether presented as promises or propaganda, would often prove as powerful as bullets.

Post–World War II, 1945–1947

When the Japanese surrendered at the end of World War II, it seemed practical and politic to allow the Japanese occupying the northern section of the Korean peninsula to surrender to the Soviet Union and for the Japanese in the southern section to surrender to the United States until elections could take place. The 38th parallel was selected as the demarcation line between the northern and southern areas of Korea in the closing hours of World War II (see map). It was a geopolitical decision that paid more heed to American and Soviet interests than to Korean social or economic balance.

The United States celebrated the close of the Second World War by welcoming returning soldiers; mourning over 400,000 combat deaths; mothballing its tanks, battleships, and bombers; and greatly reducing the size of its military. The cuts in manpower reduced or eliminated combined operations groups (both civilian and military) with experience in counterintelligence and psychological warfare. The Office of War Information (OWI) was eliminated and the Voice of America (VOA) was closeted in the State Department. The Office of Strategic Services (OSS) was closed and the small army unit at Fort Riley, Kansas, which dealt with psychological warfare, was relegated to recording the history of that type of warfare. Congress and President Harry Truman began turning the nearly 82-billion-dollar defense budget toward domestic spending.

In contrast, Soviet forces, both standard military and specialized spy and propaganda masters, never stopped refining their weapons.[2] Premier Joseph Stalin's foreign policy in its simplest form was to regain all Eastern European territories once held by the czars, bringing many of them into a Communist bloc, by force of arms if necessary, and/or replacing argumentative governments with those more compliant to the Soviet regime. In Eastern Asia, Stalin proved himself to be equally dexterous, manipulating fellow Communists as well as former allies. He ended his neutrality pact with Japan as soon as it was clear their military was buckling to Allied forces and positioned his troops to occupy land and ports promised to China.³ He held onto Manchuria and, while promising Mao Tse-tung to protect the province, had it stripped of millions of dollars worth of industrial equipment left by the Japanese. He secretly groomed Kim Il-sung for the leadership of North Korea. While Mao knew Stalin was manipulating both Chinese Nationalists and Communists strictly for Soviet gains, the young Kim Il-sung heard only Stalin's promise of the eventual reunification of the Korean peninsula made possible with the aid of Soviet arms and advisors. He never considered Stalin's deeper motives or the huge cost his country would pay.

By the summer of 1947, it was painfully clear to President Truman and his secretary of state, George C. Marshall, that the Soviet Union was no longer an ally but was a vigorous opponent who had skunked us in a new kind of war. Stalin's refusal to end his military buildup and propaganda campaign in North Korea helped bring to life the U.S. National Security Act in July 1947. The United States took Korea's case to the UN General Assembly in September of that same year. The events that followed these actions would not only have a lasting impact on the future of the Korean people, but would also affect U.S. foreign policy and military planning for the next thirty years.

The Cold War

As the Koreans struggled to find a unified voice and elect leaders, upper-level officials of the executive branch of government in Washington, DC (presidential cabinet and Pentagon) were forming a National Security Council (NSC) to carry out the provisions set forth in the National Security Act. The National Security Council was designed to coordinate the planning and analysis of civilian and military intelligence. The resulting consensus was written as a directive and delivered to President Truman as an aid in the final formulation of U.S. foreign policy and military strategy. The president then signified his formal approval of NSC directives by signing and codifying them. The early directives of the NSC reflect Washington's growing concern with the success of Soviet propaganda.

National Security Council Directives NSC/4 and 4A, issued December 19, 1947, not only required the assistant secretary of state for public affairs to coordinate anti-Communist propaganda programs of the Voice of America (VOA) with assistant secretaries of the army, navy, and air force, but also allowed overt VOA programming to supplement covert psychological operations by requiring coordination with the deputy director of the Central Intelligence Agency (CIA). Although Secretary of State George Marshall disdained the use of

propaganda, the view of his colleagues on the National Security Council pre-
vailed. It was their opinion that Soviet propaganda had left the U.S. government
"no choice but to adopt methods previously reserved for wartime" (Krugler
2000). By June 1948, National Security Counsel directives had become more
pointed. NSC Directive 10/2 aimed U.S. propaganda efforts directly at "vicious"
covert activities of the USSR and its satellite countries, which were attempting to
"discredit" and defeat the aims and activities of the United States. Psychological
warfare and special operations programs went through name changes and
departmental redescriptions to cover their activities. Some disappeared com-
pletely in the deliberate obfuscation of NSC Directive 10/2, which allowed some
operations to be "so planned and executed that any US government responsibility for them is not evident to unauthorized persons" (Nelson 1997).

The term "psychological warfare" (PW), essentially describing the creation
and use of propaganda, suddenly cropped up on top-level paperwork from the
Department of Defense and Joint Chiefs to the State Department. The air force,
which had been separated from the army to become an independent branch
of the military in July 1947 (the same date the Central Intelligence Agency
was formed), was determined not to be just a junior partner and source of
pilots and aircraft for army and CIA covert missions. They began to imple-
ment research conducted by their RAND Corporation think tank and to offer
psychological warfare training at the Air University on Maxwell Air Force Base
in Montgomery, Alabama. There, newly commissioned second lieutenants
choosing to become psychological warfare officers embarked upon a course
of training estimated to take ten years. It was anticipated that by 1950 eight
PW officers, ranking from captain to colonel, would be available. Troop space
for one PW officer per command was allocated to seven major air force commands (Johnson n.d.).

In mid-1948 Colonel Monro MacCloskey recommended that complete
units composed of psychological warfare specialists be formed. The missions
of these units would include air resupply (providing partisan support behind
enemy lines and agent insertion and retrieval capabilities) as well as communications (providing transmission and production of broadcast information and
leaflet design and delivery capabilities). By pointing the air force's psychological warfare program in this direction, Colonel MacCloskey, whose combat experience during World War II included the command of a Carpetbagger squadron,
created a military platform that was flexible enough to support civilian (CIA)
covert operations. MacCloskey's recommendations combined with the CIA's
requests to the NSC and Department of Defense for military support would
lead to the activation of the Air Resupply and Communications Service in 1951.
Colonel MacCloskey would take command of ARCS in 1952.

Throughout 1949 the United States found itself playing a game of foreign policy racquetball with Stalin's juggernaut of force and propaganda. In January 1949 General Douglas MacArthur, commander in chief, U.S. Far East Command, Headquarters Tokyo, recommended the removal of all U.S. combat forces from South Korea. In July 1949 U.S. troops were removed from South Korea, leaving behind a force of five hundred officers and men known as the Korean Military Advisory Group (KMAG). This group of soldiers, airmen, and marines were to advise the South Korean army, whose main task at the time was to maintain order within the newly formed Republic of South Korea. The Republic of Korea (ROK) Army, a force of around 98,000 soldiers, was armed only with carbines and M-1 rifles, obsolescent artillery, and light planes intended for reconnaissance. Both weaponry and troop size were kept below the level repeatedly requested by both Major General William Roberts, commander of the KMAG forces, and the American ambassador to Korea, John Muccio.

In 1949, most U.S. military and diplomatic activity was concentrated on containing Soviet advances in Eastern Europe. A steady stream of U.S. aircraft kept Berlin's blockaded civilians supplied from above the Soviet-wrought Iron Curtain. The Voice of America broadcast through the "Static Curtain" produced by Soviet jamming of broadcasts. The CIA was concerned that Soviet jamming technology was reaching a point where it would not only silence international broadcasting but could block our signals intercept program and eventually affect telecommunications worldwide. That kind of control would give Stalin more leverage than the atom bomb.

Events in East Asia were monitored with growing concern. By the end of 1949, Chairman Mao Tse-tung had emerged as the leader of China and Generalissimo Chiang Kai-shek's Nationalists were forced off the mainland to the island of Taiwan. Mao and Stalin had signed a Sino-Soviet Treaty linking Mao's massive Communist army with Stalin's advanced weaponry. Korea had been split into North and South, with Kim Il-sung named premier of North Korea without UN oversight. Syngman Rhee had been elected president of South Korea in elections monitored by the United Nations Temporary Commission on Korea (UNTCOK). Additionally, CIA, army, and air force reports all concurred that Stalin had given the Soviet-appointed Kim Il-sung the go-ahead to attack South Korea and was supplying the North Korean Peoples' Army (NKPA) with arms and equipment.

In January 1950, the U.S. National Security Council began work on NSC Directive 68, which called for a buildup of *all* U.S. military forces, from the refinement of the hydrogen bomb to the authorization of special operations wings to include psychological warfare units. However, without a hot conflict to focus funding, work continued mainly on paper (and at Washington speed). In an effort to eliminate possible leaks of sensitive defense information outlined in Directive 68, council members issued directives designed to protect sources and intelligence-gathering activities. The bureaucracy of secrecy was growing and the air force's newly created Psychological Warfare Division scoured all air force personnel listings to find Washington-savvy, ranking officers with any understanding of unconventional warfare to represent it on the continually shifting committees and boards that controlled not only information but defense budget allocations.

When the NSC received confirmation that parts of Directive 68 were being leaked to Moscow almost as quickly as they were written, council members crafted certain passages deliberately for eyes in the Kremlin and secreted others. The knowledge that prompted this unusual approach of communicating vital information to the Soviets via their spies in the higher echelons of U.S. intelligence came from a U.S. Army Central Intelligence Corps breakthrough in interception and decoding of Russian transmissions. Though President Truman would not receive NSC Directive 68 for final authorization until August 1950 (and it would be considered classified information in the United States for the next twenty-five years), both Moscow and Washington would use portions of it to guide State and military responses throughout the Korean War.

In the spring of 1950, both President Truman and his new secretary of state, Dean Acheson, continued to speak openly about the perils of communism. News of heightened U.S. military activity was kept prominent. The USAF announced that the Military Air Transport Service (MATS) was being revamped, doubling the number of air crews available for service in "time of need." The U.S. Seventh Fleet and British naval forces were in joint exercises, and the first-line U.S. carriers *Valley Forge* and *Boxer* were rotated to keep the U.S. flag visible in southeast Asia at all times. Marine units practiced amphibious assaults and navy frogmen drilled with U.S. Eighth Army troops in Japan. Coverage of Chinese Communist forces massing to attack Taiwan was aired abroad by the VOA and by media sources in the United States. Yet news of Soviet arms buildup in Korea was hard to find anywhere, although small teams of U.S. operatives continued to relay descriptions of extensive battle preparations by North Korean forces from Tokyo and Seoul through select channels to Washington.

The Unexpected War

In the United States it was midday, June 24, 1950, as President Truman's plane flew slightly north of the 38th parallel carrying him home from the East Coast to Independence, Missouri. Fourteen hours ahead, it was just after midnight along the 38th parallel in Korea. In some areas a steady rain dampened soldiers of three ROK divisions patrolling the boundary. Perhaps the weather muffled the final approach of the Soviet-made T-34 tanks, or perhaps sentries, numbed from constant harassment and raids from the north, dreamed about their homes and farms to the south. East again and north of the 38th in Tokyo, General Douglas MacArthur was sleeping soundly at his headquarters. If his sleep was troubled by anything, it was troop cuts Washington was making in his Far East Command.

Master Sergeant Donald Nichols (later to be promoted to Warrant Officer then to Major), known as "Mr." Nichols, worked feverishly through that night at Kimpo Airfield outside Seoul. He was keenly aware of the depth, strength, and intention of the North Korean army divisions massing along the 38th parallel and had sent a specific warning to the Far East Command in Tokyo. (Throughout the conflict in Korea Nichols continued to organize and lead Korean partisans in covert military operations. Handling Korean agents gathering what he termed "positive intelligence," Mr. Nichols became, by action rather than intent, the founding father of the U.S. Air Force human intelligence programs.) North Korean army forces rolled into the outskirts of Seoul with a speed that amazed even the Russian officers who planned the advance. Nichols sent his men, along with the thousands of distraught civilians and the broken military units seeking refuge, south of the Han River. His last report, Sunday morning, June 25, 1950, gave the U.S. Far East Air Force headquarters in Tokyo its first official notification the war had started.

Truman's return to Washington on that same Sunday morning, rather than Saturday evening when he was first notified of the attack in Korea, was orchestrated by Secretary of State Dean Acheson, who worked quickly in the interim to prepare and inform certain upper-level government personnel. As planned, the president's arrival raised few alarms. Phone wires and telecable transmissions hummed into and around Washington as an emergency assembly of the UN Security Council was called, but that morning the press was quiet, save for a brief mention on page 20 of the *New York Times*, which carried a stinging rebuke from Secretary of Defense Louis Johnson and comments from the State Department accusing the Soviet Union of backing the attack on South Korea.

United Nations Police Action in Korea

Late that afternoon on June 25, 1950, on the basis of reports from the United Nations Temporary Commission on Korea (UNTCOK) and information from the U.S. ambassador to Korea, the UN Security Council voted unanimously to accept the resolution calling for immediate cessation of hostilities and North Korean troop withdrawal to the 38th parallel.[4] An increasingly bloody advance by North Korean troops toward the southern tip of Korea prompted the United Nations to respond with an additional resolution on the 27th of June. Member nations were called upon to render assistance to the Republic of Korea in any way necessary to repel the attack and restore international peace and security to the area. The "unexpected war" now became, according to President Truman, a United Nations Police Action. Seventeen nations would send a combined total of over 900,000 troops to Korea as part of the UN Command. Five more would provide medical assistance. By the time armistice was declared in July 1953, the United States would commit over 300,000 combat forces to the conflict (Bennett and Madden 2003).

At the outbreak of the Korean War, backing for Truman's decision to support the Republic of Korea and enforce the UN resolution with American troops had strong public support in the United States and abroad. However, the president and Secretary of State Acheson would have to do some damage control in the face of the complete "surprise" attack in Korea. The director of the CIA was fired. Army Chief of Staff and Commander in Chief of the Joint Chiefs of Staff General Omar N. Bradley assessed that the only remotely combat-ready division in the army at the outbreak of the war was the Eighty-second Airborne. The marine corps listed 98,000 men, down from 480,000 in 1948. The navy, which had seen a reduction of nearly 90 percent of its action force, was down to 15 aircraft carriers and a destroyer force of 137 ships. The young air force held only forty-eight groups of a command recommendation of seventy groups. The United States would begin rearmament immediately.

If projection forces (navy and air force) and ground forces had fallen to budget cuts, psychological warfare branches had become nearly extinct. Special operations units had not been formed. The Far East Command held a "Special Projects Division" couched under G2 (Intelligence Directorate) with Colonel J. Woodall Greene in charge. Greene, who had been an executive officer with five hundred soldiers in his Psychological Warfare Branch (PWB) at the end of World War II, now at the outbreak of the Korean War had a staff of two officers and two civilians. Their advantage was they had been planning psywar operations in the event of attacks in Korea since 1947. On June 27, 1950, President Truman authorized air operations south of the 38th parallel. On June 28, 12 million leaflets produced by Greene's PWB, printed by Japanese firms and delivered by the U.S. Air Force, fluttered through the skies over Korea with the message "Resist the Communists—Help is on the way." Radio stations in Japan started to broadcast messages into Communist-held

areas a short time later. Colonel Greene's Psychological Warfare Branch would
expand to thirty-five in the first six months of the war, and the branch would
be upgraded and transferred to Far East Command's Operations Directorate in
1952. The Far East Command's PW Section would act as the UN Command's
coordinating agency for Korean tactical and strategic-level psychological warfare operations throughout the war.

By June 29 the North Korean Peoples' Army was in control of Seoul.
Scattered elements of the South Korean Army (ROK) and their KMAG advisors
fought desperately to keep NKPA units from pushing south across the Han
River. General Douglas MacArthur, who had been getting dire reports from
remnant forces on the ground, flew to Korea. He landed at Suwon Airfield
twenty miles south of Seoul as B-29s dropped 500-pound bombs on Kimpo
Airfield and on major Seoul train stations in an effort to stall the enemy advance.
Once situated on a hilltop, he could see the devastation in Seoul. Viewing the
ragged, exhausted soldiers trailing south and the spearhead approach of NKPA
tanks, MacArthur lowered his field glasses, nodded toward the last railroad
bridge running south from the besieged South Korean capital, and gave the
order to take it out. In four days MacArthur had gone from having no policy
for action in Korea, to promising arms to control a border skirmish, to ordering
bomb strikes on airfields north of the 38th parallel, to realizing he would have
to commit almost all of the American occupation force (Eighth Army) in Japan
just to hang onto Korea. Truman authorized the bombing of North Korea and a
sea blockade of the Korean coast on June 29 and the next day gave authorization to send U.S. ground troops to Korea.

MacArthur was not the only commander of forces in Korea to be con-
fronted with international strategies running counter to his plans. On Monday,
June 26, the twenty-eight-year-old Kim Il-sung, premier of North Korea, broadcast from the North Korean capital of Pyŏngyang (see map). Students were
called to assemblies to listen to their premier and commander in chief of the
North Korean Peoples Army. The students were anxious and puzzled. Friends
and family members had been ordered to prepare for military exercises, and
then they disappeared. Radios and newspapers were not allowed in the college
dormitories. Students were eager for information. Kim Il-sung told them North
Korea had been forced to wage a just war for freedom, democracy, unification,
and independence of the motherland. Their leader left little doubt that North
Korea had been attacked by South Korea, whose corrupt president was a pawn
of the American imperialists. Few listening to his speech ever questioned that
the attack had come from South Korea. The fiery anti-Communist rhetoric of
South Korea's President Syngman Rhee was so strong that even veteran U.S.
reporters in Tokyo with cable and broadcast news access questioned who had

initiated the attack. (The autocratic Rhee was often as much a challenge to the U.S. military and State sponsors of his South Korean government as he was a staunch ally because of his insistence on continually attacking Communist-controlled North Korea [Toland 1991]. As late as 1954 Syngman Rhee, then on tour in the United States, claimed to have started the war in Korea in hopes of destroying communism [Pickering 1991; Easton 1968].)

By June 29, Premier Kim Il-sung, whose 150,000 troops had crossed the 38th parallel on June 25 with the help of an estimated 3,000 Soviet officers, equipment, and communications, found his command in Seoul victorious, but without its Soviet advisors. In addition to relying heavily on Soviet military leadership and communications, Kim Il-sung had been encouraged to believe some 200,000 South Korean Workers Party members in hiding would revolt, toppling the South Korean regime. Propaganda leaflets from the North voiced the virtue and humanity of the NKPA and its Russian helpers. "Have no fear!" they assured the people. The kind and merciful forces of Kim Il-sung would help free them from the American oppressors who were now allies of the hated Japanese. But no riots occurred, not even one that would have thrown the docks of Pusan, Korea's largest port and only UN Command toehold on the peninsula, into chaos. Kim purged his propaganda controller and pleaded with Stalin for more arms and Russian advisors to organize a battle plan for the push to Pusan.

Stalin did not consider the taking of Pusan a priority. His careful handling of the ambitious Kim Il-sung had less to do with strengthening Communist control in Korea than with weakening Chinese Communist efforts to form any alliance with the United States. As far as Stalin was concerned, the weaker China was, the safer Russia was. The best way to deplete Chinese strength was to push Mao into war with the United Nations in general and the United States in particular. So the Soviet-backed North Korean force that could have ended the war in the summer of 1950 by pushing through to Pusan stalled as Kim Il-sung waited in Seoul for directions from Moscow. American journalists positioned south of the Han River to cover the action as Kim pushed along the Seoul-Pusan corridor could comment only on the quiet.

MacArthur was named Supreme Commander of UN forces in Korea on July 7, 1950. That same day Mao, who realized his hope for the "reunification of Taiwan" using Soviet-supplied weaponry was lost because Stalin had backed Kim Il-sung's advance into South Korea,[5] and who was in no mood to appear to be Stalin's puppet, nonetheless began gradually moving troops that had been poised to attack Taiwan north toward the Chinese–North Korean border. The Chinese Peoples Central Committee, realizing a Communist Korea allied with China rather than the Soviet Union or under

UN oversight would be in their best interest, established a Northern Border Defense Army (BDA). By the end of July 1950 Chinese troop strength along the Sino-Korean border doubled to 260,000 troops. The U.S. Joint Chiefs estimated the battle-hardened troops led by some of Mao's best commanders could reach the port of Pusan in five days, in the process sweeping the president and governing assembly of South Korea, entire divisions of the Eighth Army, and the UN Command Forces landing at Pusan off the Korean peninsula (see map).

There was frantic diplomatic and military activity in Washington and Moscow in an effort to control Mao's decision on when and how to use his Border Defense Army. Stalin offered more jets and pilots to cover Mao's forces if they advanced into Korea. The U.S. National Security Council Directive 76 for troop withdrawal from the Korean peninsula and activation of contingency plans for World War III was codified and leaked to Moscow. Truman ordered a flight of nuclear-configured B-29s to Guam. MacArthur decided to meet with Chiang Kai-shek to offer assistance and assurance in the defense of Taiwan, as many in the Department of Defense favored using Taiwan as a U.S. base for attacking mainland China.

By the end of July and into August, not only did the chaos and desperation on the ground in Korea increase, the fear and confusion in Washington was palpable. Secretary of State Dean Acheson had to make clear to President Truman that threats against Mao and the Chinese Communists might look good in the American papers but if they precipitated China's intervention in the Korean conflict before UN Command Forces had been deployed, the result would be disastrous militarily as well as diplomatically. Once Acheson got the agreement and cooperation of the president, the State Department and the Department of Defense work could begin on reining in MacArthur, Chiang Kai-shek—who was using U.S.-supplied planes to sink Chinese Communist ships—and the VOA, which was broadcasting anti-Communist information on Mao's crippling taxes and land appropriations necessary to support his Border Defense Army. It didn't help that the Soviet ambassador to the United Nations, Jacob Malik, had returned in August as president of the UN Security Council and was using his position to push member nations to drop participation in the Korean Police Action and to admit Communist China to the United Nations.

The offices of diplomats, ambassadors, State Department staffers, and military liaisons worked every channel available to repair the blowback from the ill-timed poke at China. From New York to Washington, London to Paris, Moscow to Beijing, and New Delhi to Tokyo, the United States responded to assure the world they had no intention of attacking mainland China. Truman called the B-29s back from Guam and directly rebuked MacArthur. Chiang

Kai-shek was told "diplomatically" to stop threatening to attack mainland China with U.S. arms and equipment. It was arranged for the careful K. M. Panikkar, India's ambassador to China, to assure Mao that channels were open for trade and treaties with the United States. Mao sent only a small force across the northern border. His Chinese soldiers, who were purposefully "designed for capture," carried complete identification papers that served as their message to POW interrogators of the UN Command that Chinese forces were in Korea. Otherwise, he continued to barter with Stalin, the United States, and the UN. Other than Malik's harangues as the president of the UN Security Council, Moscow was strangely quiet. The Russian Bear, having devoured parts of Europe, the Middle East, and East Asia, seemed to be napping.

Even without overt support from the Soviets, Kim Il-sung's NKPA was pushing toward Pusan. Though their human wave of infantry advanced in fits and starts and had been compared by Russian officers to a windup toy, their advances proved to be devastating for undermanned South Korean troops and hastily organized Eighth Army task forces trying to hold ground in the South. Haunting images of exhausted, broken troops accompanied stories in publications from Seattle to New York, as Lieutenant General Walton Walker, commander of the U.S. Eighth Army in Korea, pulled forces together to defend Pusan. By jeep, driven only slightly slower than a light plane could fly, Walker visited his troops. He constantly analyzed both victories and defeats including those resulting from his own misjudgments. The reports of General Walker's heroic efforts to keep a perimeter around Pusan left little doubt of the grim situation. The press would nickname Walker "Bulldog." Patton had labeled him "a fighting son of a bitch" during the invasion of Normandy in World War II. Fortunately for the Eighth Army and the UN military units deploying to Pusan, he was both, as the battles to hold the Pusan perimeter called for the seasoned strategies and courageous tenacity of a veteran commander.

In addition to scattered units fighting guerilla-style from ridgelines and craggy defiles, and brigades with tanks and artillery dug in to hold roads and river crossings, there were a half-million homeless refugees streaming south to seek protection in UN-held territory. The American ambassador, John Muccio, and his staff were as busy getting panicked South Korean refugees settled and reassured as Walker's officers were organizing a multinational, combined-force defense under chaotic and desperate circumstances. Trying to be as upbeat as the leaflets illustrating the strength and kindness of UN forces coming to South Korea's aid, Muccio also had to prepare President Syngman Rhee and Madame Rhee to evacuate once again, this time to the safety of an island off the peninsula. At nearly eighty years of age the autocratic Rhee, who was known to close staff as the "Old Revolutionary," drew his pistol on Muccio and told him that if the enemy broke in he would shoot his wife first and then himself, but he would not leave Korea.

On September 15, after battling the Joint Chiefs of Staff and ignoring Typhoon Kezia, General MacArthur launched his amphibious attack on Inchon with considerable assistance from naval intelligence, language specialists, the CIA, and South Korean agents in addition to firepower borrowed from General Walker's defense of Pusan. It was a "no written orders" secret for U.S. military, but Mao, who had studied the tide tables and understood MacArthur as well as the rough west coast of Korea, had sent warning to Kim Il-sung, as had North Korean intelligence officers who had seen the massing of ships off the coast west of Seoul. A savvy Associated Press correspondent extracted the landing date and location from an ROK officer celebrating a victory over the NKPA near Pusan. He filed his story through Tokyo before the Joint Chiefs got MacArthur's final plan.

By September 29 the Inchon-Seoul area was under control of elements of the Fifth Marine Regiment and the Eighth Army X Corps. MacArthur returned Seoul to Syngman Rhee and the ROK Army. Pusan was secured. Still, survival trumped organizational charting as General Walker added whatever forces he needed wherever he needed them to hold the 141-mile line around Pusan and begin the move north, a plan designed to trap remaining NKPA soldiers between Pusan and UN Command forces ranging east from Seoul. Some decimated U.S. Army units had to add as many as one hundred Korean soldiers per company, many of whom were only fifteen years old.[6] The British Twenty-seventh Brigade, rushed from Hong Kong and later augmented by an Australian battalion, became the Twenty-seventh British Commonwealth Brigade and marched north into the Korean mountains still in their jungle fatigues.

Covert operations covering the kaleidoscopic battle plans in Korea during the first six months of the war were equally free from an overburden of written regulations and organizational description. Outfits such as the Far East Command's "Liaison Group" (FEC/LG) seemed to form around high-priority combat problems the way fast-moving Korean weather could move in and off a ridgeline—one minute there, gone the next. Though their missions were often similar (insertion of spies in seemingly every nook and cranny of the enemy's domain and retrieval of that information and those individuals from behind enemy lines as well as delivery of the psywar message by leaflet and loudspeaker), group names and specialists varied widely. Unconventional warfare was a work in progress, and as General Walker adjusted his forces by need to defend Pusan, so special operations teams and ad hoc liaisons grew up to be adjusted and named later as needed.

Pilots of Unit 4 belonging to the 315th Air Division headquartered in Tokyo had from the outset of war spent so much time in flights over both

North and South Korea they were nicknamed "Kyushu Gypsies." From fields as close to the battlefront as they could land their C-47s, Unit 4 moved from the Japanese island of Kyushu with the troops moving north from Pusan, to Taegu Air Field (UN designate K-2), then Kimpo Air Field (K-14), and back to Taegu. In February 1951, Unit 4's activities of agent insertion and psywar support would see formal activation in the establishment of a Special Air Missions (SAM) Detachment at Taegu South Airfield. By delivering everyone from partisans to visiting Pentagon brass to downed pilots, and by carrying everything from leaflets to loudspeakers, SAM air crews provided air force psychological warfare planners headquartered in Washington ample illustrations of the strengths as well as the weaknesses of combat special operations.

As the Air Force Psychological Warfare Division went into high gear to train psywar officers, UN Command Forces moved north of the 38th parallel. On September 30, 1950, the ROK Third Division crossed the 38th parallel intent on pushing north to reunify Korea. President Truman's authorization for action in the north had come on the 27th and the UN resolution for action supporting reunification followed on October 7. Premier Mao Tse-tung, deciding to commit his forces in order to keep North Korea in the Asian Communist bloc, declared on October 4, 1950, that the Chinese Peoples Volunteer Army would fight alongside the North Korean Army.

In Tokyo a shortage of planes as well as pilots meant that U.S. Fifth Air Force pilots flew whatever got the job done for whichever branch of the military had aircraft available. Air force pilots flying Air Materiel Command "Voice" C-47s equipped with loudspeakers began flights to induce enemy surrenders. The speakers were heavy and ineffective at speeds or altitudes that would protect the aircraft from ground fire. However, when flown "on the deck" by ingenious, determined crews, the "Voice" C-47s proved to be both intimidating and demoralizing and were effective in cinching surrenders. The early missions also resulted in improved speaker design. By the end of November, the U.S. Air Force had six psychological warfare officers split between the Far East Command PW Joint Staff and the G-2 PW Branch of Far East Air Force Headquarters. Japan-based army and air force leafleteers were turning out hundreds of millions of leaflets, but the limited number of C-47s and qualified pilots held leafleting missions to two or three a week. As the UN forces moved deeper into North Korea under orders to secure all of Korea, long-range B-29s covered their advance to the Manchurian border, and intramural spats over whether they would be used to deliver bombs or leaflets tended to be won by bomb delivery.

The other air war heating up at that time did not need to wait for planes to deliver its weapons. The U.S. Army Tactical Information Department (TID) left Fort Riley, Kansas, on September 9 and arrived in Pusan on October 15,

1950. Composed of four officers and twenty men, it was redesignated the First Loudspeaker and Leaflet Company. Nicknamed the "Proper Ganders," with a top-hat-wearing gander as its unit symbol, the mobile company would cover tactical psychological warfare for the Eighth Army (Jones 2007).

Additionally, from permanent transmitters located throughout Japan, broadcasts prepared at the Armed Forces Radio Station in Tokyo by Voice of UN Command (VUNC) carried the UN slant on the war in Korean, Chinese, and English. This broadcast arm of psywar was aimed at an estimated 100,000 North Korean listeners as well as South Korean military and civilian groups. With the addition of Koreans formerly employed by the Korean National Broadcasting System, VUNC was able to get programs out twenty-four hours a day on multiple frequencies. In October 1950, UN Command forces occupied the North Korean capital of Pyŏngyang and the VUNC team took special delight in broadcasting anti-Communist programs from what had been the major Communist broadcast link in Korea. Their work in Pyŏngyang, however, would be cut short. The UN Command's occupation of North Korea would last only through December, as divided elements of the UN forces, including entire divisions of the U.S. Eighth Army and the Republic of South Korean Army, were swept back to the south by the Chinese Peoples Volunteer Army and rejuvenated North Korean troops.

The opening months of 1951 saw the UN Command back on the defensive. General MacArthur's orders to Lieutenant General Walker changed from advance and mop up fleeing North Korean forces as far north as the Yalu River (see map) to "give up territory if you have to, but save the Eighth Army." Lieutenant General Walker was killed organizing the defense of Seoul and Lieutenant General Matthew B. Ridgway was named to replace him as commander of the Eighth Army. UN Command Forces evacuated the South Korean capital of Seoul on January 4, 1951, and with MacArthur's consent, Ridgway pulled his UN Command into more defensible positions across the narrow waist of the Korean Peninsula south of the 38th parallel. Psychological warfare units attached to both the Fifth Air Force and the Eighth Army pulled back as well, leaving as little evidence of their activities or useful equipment as possible.

Air Resupply and Communications Service — Unconventional War

Almost before airmen knew their uniforms would be blue, the intelligence branch of the newly formed air force began to plan for an unconventional warfare wing that would combine the capabilities of partisan support and psychological warfare. In February 1951, the Joint Chiefs of Staff gave the job to the air force and the Air Resupply and Communications Service (ARCS)

was activated at Andrews Air Force Base, Military Air Transport Service Headquarters, on the outskirts of Washington, DC. The Military Air Transport
Service was assigned to organize, instruct, and equip personnel necessary for
the air support side of the command. However, the ARCS wings were also the
operational arms of the Air Force Psychological Warfare Division. This dual
command solution to forming a new service meant the 581st Air Resupply and
Communications Wing operating from Clark Air Base in the Philippines would
be able to get mission clearance straight from Washington. In theory, this solution would enable a quicker response time and improve their ability to keep a
lower profile than they would have by passing plans through the vetting of the
Far East Command. Not surprisingly, Fifth Air Force officers in Korea, trying
to coordinate everything from payroll to daily orders and the assignment of
quarters for air force additions to their ranks, tagged those claiming to belong
to the mysterious 581st as belonging to the "Pentagon's Wing."

The 581st ARCS Wing was activated at Mountain Home Air Force Base,
Idaho, on a "skeleton basis" on July 23, 1951. "Advanced instruction" is as
mild a description of the intense and diverse training that ARCS wing officers
underwent as "air base" is for the remote, abandoned World War II facility
that faced them at Mountain Home, Idaho. Though the isolated stretch of
Idaho was a fine place to hide air force secret activity, the training necessary
to prepare wing officers would see them more often away from Mountain
Home than present. Upon completion of basic courses at Georgetown, officers
would be apprenticed in specialties. The Voice of America in New York and
Radio Munich in Germany accepted ARCS trainees in broadcasting. The Army
General School at Fort Riley, Kansas, gave ARCS officers extended journalism and propaganda training. Specific courses in languages and regional dia-
lects were arranged through a combination of military and civilian institutions
and agencies such as the Army Language School in Monterey, California, and
American University in Beirut, Lebanon. Officers choosing the line of ARCS
assignments most carefully buried in secrecy (Holding and Briefing Squadron)
received Special Forces guerrilla training at Fort Benning, Georgia. Pilot and
crew training in the combined aircraft belonging to the Air Resupply Squadrons
of ARCS was rigorous, hair-raising, and in some cases deadly. The World War
II–era B-29 Superfortress heavy bomber, key to ARCS long-range penetration
of enemy territory, had to be pulled out of mothballs and refitted to deliver
agents and leaflets. Not only did pilots need to adjust to low-level, nearly stall-
speed flight, they had to practice at night. Experienced air crews were next to
impossible to pry from older, more traditional air force commands. Continual
requests from the fledgling ARCS wings for a training squadron to be sent to
Mountain Home resulted in the arrival of one instructor from MATS.

From the beginning of their training, all Air Resupply and Communications Service personnel were taught that secrecy was a key element in the success of their missions. Lessons at Georgetown and the VOA encouraged students to become critical consumers of media, for world opinion rested on information. The trick was to "contour" the flow of information gathered from both open and covert sources. ARCS propaganda endeavors were focused on gathering information and delivering it in a manner that would do the most good for America's interests. Accordingly, the 581st ARCS Wing (which would eventually be deployed to the Philippines) had within its command six distinct squadrons, some deeply secret and some as open as the daily news, all aware their weapon would be information and their shield would be secrecy.

Korea-Stalemate

On March 15, 1951, Seoul was retaken by forces of the UN Command. The city had been occupied by opposing armies four times in less than one year. In the rubble of the few remaining buildings, roughly 200,000 of the city's original 1,500,000 citizens hung on without light or water and very little food. The Eighth Army, ROK, and UN Command Forces in General Ridgway's operations code-named "Killer" and "Ripper" had pushed Chinese and North Korean forces back to the north and solidified a defense across the width of the peninsula at roughly the 38th parallel. In that spring of 1951, the human cost of the war was impossible to hide as thawing hills gave up their dead. Thousands of dead Chinese Army soldiers whose cotton-padded uniforms had frozen to their bodies, locking them in the winter snows, came down in snowmelt streams, blocking fields and shorelines. The feces-fertilized rice paddies also stank of rotting flesh as the warm rains turned fields and roads into impassable bogs. For North Korean civilians facing starvation, the loss of farms, fields, and factories, and the pollution of thousands of dead left unburied, the fear of deadly disease was greater than that of any bombardment.

Fifteen hundred Chinese troops had been reported to be seriously affected by disease in the areas of North Korea close to the Manchurian border. (In March 1951, Brigadier General Crawford Sams, with the support of Korean agents and partisans, reached and examined gravely ill North Korean and Chinese soldiers behind enemy lines in North Korea. Sams verified outbreaks of both typhus and hemorrhagic smallpox, diseases endemic in Manchuria. He found neither the bubonic or septicemic forms of plague.) Despite the open publication of General Sams' report, blame for the deaths of both soldiers and civilians would be placed squarely on the United States by Chinese and Soviet ambassadors familiar not only with the diseases that ravaged their countries due to their own harsh regimes, but with the power of psychological warfare. Communist Party officers assigned to North Korean and Chinese combat units continued to tell their soldiers that UN "Safe Surrender" leaflets were covered with deadly bacteria.

From the military point of view, the ugliness of the Korean conflict, which had bogged down in a stalemate of wrangling, truce talks, and deadly skirmishes for bits of territory along the Main Line of Resistance (MLR), was that it was being conducted as an ideological showcase or State-run negotiation. MacArthur was hardly alone when he endorsed attacking China from Taiwan or through Manchuria, nor was he alone in thinking that Russia, should it be bold enough to strike in Korea, could be beaten. However, he was on his own when as the supreme commander of the UN forces in Korea, he went to the press and repeatedly endorsed his opinions, and when he contacted congressional representatives to express his views in Congress. On April 11, 1951, General Douglas MacArthur was relieved of his command by President Truman. Lieutenant General Matthew Ridgway was named supreme commander. Though he agreed with MacArthur, as did the Joint Chiefs and the secretary of the army, they also understood that the president was the commander in chief of the military. Another general would win the presidency in November 1952, and his promise was not to extend the war beyond Korea but to end it.

The opening of peace talks proposed by the Soviet ambassador to the United Nations, Jacob Malik, began in July 1951 in Kaesong. Neither Chinese, North Korean, nor American military leaders were in the habit of trusting the Soviets, but the brutal conflict now being played to the world audience by hundreds of journalists in Korea required a response from both Communist and independent nations. The Soviets had a win-win situation with the Chinese and UN forces weakening each other while they got the propaganda benefits of being the concerned neighbor. The peace talks begun in July in Kaesong sputtered to a halt, not to resume until October 1951. In 1952 the fighting in Korea continued to be as stalemated and deadly as the trench warfare of World War I. Peace talks were deadlocked, verbally violent, and unproductive.

The 581st in Korea

The 581st ARCS Wing received orders to report to Clark Air Force Base in the Philippines in July 1952, only one year after their shoestring activation at Mountain Home. Here, pilots, crews, and psychological warfare officers would receive assignments and training relevant to the Far East. Though the majority of the 581st assignments would send men and aircraft to the hot war of Korea, some would rotate to Indochina and some would be reserved for CIA business outside the Department of Defense. As the 581st commander, Colonel John K. Arnold Jr. met with the Far East Air Force staff to form an operations plan for his composite wing. His emphasis would be on the flexibility of his personnel and aircraft and on the need for the discrete dispersal of covert personnel and weaponry. Colonel Arnold's ARCS wing, offering a range of unconventional weaponry, read like a wish list for commanders with missions along the jagged coastlines and unforgiving mountainous terrain of North Korea. Men and equipment were quickly parceled out (Haas 1997).

Pilots, mechanics, and psychological warfare officers from the 581st ARCS Wing were rotated into the war zone in small groups, to receive "on-the-job" training under the command of the Eighth Army or Fifth Air Force. In the summer of 1952, the "Spook City" portion of Seoul City Air Base (K-16) was filled with aircraft painted black or dull gray that came and went in the dark. However, even though hidden by a twisted command trail, some ARCS pilots, their aircraft, and their missions were as plain to Communist spies as the outlines of a B-29. Colonel John Arnold's B-29 Superfortress, call sign *Stardust 40*, flying out of Yokota, Japan, for the Ninety-first Reconnaissance Squadron, was reported missing in action during a routine leaflet drop near the Manchurian/North Korean border on January 15, 1953. In less than a year from its deployment to the Philippines, the 581st had to adjust to the facts that its commander was a Chinese prisoner of war and that its covert status had been seriously compromised.

POWs and the Politics of Peace

General Dwight Eisenhower visited his son, Major John Eisenhower, in the summer of 1952 after being given the Republican Party nomination for president. On that visit he cautioned John, who was to take command of a battalion along the front in Korea, against being taken prisoner. He promised to terminate his presidential campaign if John were captured. The Communists were playing to a world audience. Any confession they could wring out of captured officers was priceless propaganda. The son of a presidential candidate would present them with an opportunity for crippling blackmail. Soviet and Chinese Communist envoys continually pressured the United Nations to punish the United States for its alleged use of germ warfare by producing confessions signed by captured pilots admitting to the use of biological weapons. The United States had no defense except to say it had not used such weapons.

Forty-five percent of American lives lost during the Korean conflict were taken in the battles to hold territory along the MLR near the 38th parallel. The peace talks continued into 1953 and focused more closely on the return of prisoners of war. The exchange-of-prisoners issue would haunt the UN negotiators through the winter and into the spring of 1953. President Eisenhower faced the same dilemma President Truman had in 1951 when he insisted that prisoners be given the right to resist repatriation to Communist-held countries against their will. Additionally, Eisenhower had to battle his own secretary of state, John Foster Dulles, who advanced the National Security Council argument that the United States had to continue its confrontation of communism globally with armed diplomacy, knowing full well what all the wrangling was costing daily in American lives.

The leaflet and loudspeaker campaigns, which encouraged surrender by supplying ragged, starving North Korean and Chinese soldiers with safe conduct passes and instructions on escape, had been instrumental in the UN Command capture of over 100,000 prisoners of war. The Chinese list of Allied prisoners showed one tenth as many. They explained that the low numbers were due to the desire of "progressive" prisoners to change to the Communist side. General Mark W. Clark, supreme commander of UN forces in Korea,[7] and General Maxwell Taylor, the incoming commander of the Eighth Army, supported an increasing reliance on both partisan and psywar operations as well as on strategic bombing of factories and hydroelectric plants in North Korea in order to force the Chinese to drop demands for total POW repatriation.[8] Finally, in April 1953, Panmunjom negotiators agreed that a small number of wounded, ill, and seriously disabled prisoners would be exchanged. Generals Taylor and Clark held their operations to the existing MLR, and Mao's Commanding General Peng Ten-huai agreed to do the same. Even the Soviets, following the death of Stalin in March 1953, were looking in earnest for an end to the conflict. The British Commonwealth divisions, which were dug into bunkers and trenches often only two hundred yards from Chinese bunkers, celebrated the coronation of their beloved Queen Elizabeth II on June 2 with wild displays of colored smoke canisters fired above their lines. Even the entrenched soldiers of the Chinese Communist forces stood out to watch the show.

On June 18, 1953, the military leaders agreed to demarcation lines, and the details of a final prisoner exchange were ironed out. Peace seemed near. Then, on June 20, Syngman Rhee had 25,000 North Korean prisoners released from the UN Command POW camps. It was an act that was supported by many in the United States as well as by the unanimous consent of the South Korean Assembly. The freed North Koreans had been impressed into the military and forced to join the first wave of NKPA that had swept to the edges of Pusan in June 1950. In addition Rhee was exhorting his ROK divisions, which held more than half of the front, to push north. He was also urging his citizens to riot and to settle for nothing but the promised reunification of Korea.

The U.S. Army would suffer one thousand casualties a week in the struggles that followed the release until the final armistice on July 27, 1953. The U.S. government considered putting the plan to overthrow Rhee, which had been drawn up a year earlier, into effect. President Eisenhower told Rhee he would initiate both UN and U.S. evacuation from Korea unless the South Korean leader pulled his rioters into line with the provisions agreed to at Panmunjom. Mao, realizing that China had nothing to gain by stalling the armistice, stuck to the negotiated truce. Some of the last UN Command leaflets to flutter down along the blast-torn no-man's-land of the 38th parallel carried the doves of peace and the words "Leave Korea to the Koreans."

The Uneasy End

The ARCS experiment was deactivated January 1, 1954. Colonel Arnold and the crew of *Stardust 40* were released on August 4, 1955. In 1955 the U.S. Congress recognized the "UN Police Action" as the Korean War. Today American and UN forces still patrol the Korean Demilitarized Zone as agreed in the 1953 Mutual Defense Treaty with South Korea. The greater metropolitan area of Seoul including the port of Inchon now has a population of 23 million people, roughly half the population of South Korea—all within range of North Korean artillery.

Chapter One

Active Duty

The adventure began when, at the age of seventeen, I joined the navy, in part because of the traditional teenage longing to go to sea and in further part to avoid being drafted into the army.[1] It was the spring of 1945, and neither I nor my fellow farm boys who enlisted for similar reasons had the slightest idea that the war would be over by about the time we graduated from boot camp or that, alas, only a lucky few of us would get to go to sea. In the following fifteen months, until as a yeoman third class I was discharged honorably for "Fidelity and Obedience," I, as one of the unlucky ones, was stationed at Terminal Island Naval Base, which fronted on Los Angeles Harbor.

Out of the navy in 1946, I enrolled as a freshman that fall at the University of Washington in Seattle, where during the next four years I majored in anthropology and, most important, married the bright and beautiful Susan Lombard Horsley to whom this book is dedicated. The navy still held much appeal. The University of Washington had on its campus a naval ROTC (Reserve Officers Training Corps) unit that, as a result of the Second World War, offered former enlisted men from any branch of the service two years rather than the usual four years of university-level classes. This shortened program, if completed successfully, would earn its candidates commissions as reserve ensigns.

Naturally, I wished to apply, but to my astonishment I was told at their front desk by a large imperious civilian woman that I would not qualify because, as she noticed, my teeth did not have the proper "bite." Afterward it occurred to me that I should have insisted on seeing a navy officer about this

supposed deficiency. But intimidated as I was, I walked over to the air force
ROTC building where, after completing a similar two-year program, I was
commissioned a reserve second lieutenant on June 10, 1950.

The first shots of the Korean War were fired fifteen days later.

Unaware of the imminent outbreak of war, Sue and I, following spring
graduation in which Sue was awarded a BA and I became a reserve second
lieutenant, paid off our landlady and in anticipation of a summer on the
Columbia River, moved across the Cascades to Yakima County. Professor
Douglas Osborn, a University of Washington anthropologist, had earlier that
spring signed us on as a two-member archaeological survey crew to explore
a stretch of the river's basin that in the near future was to be flooded by the
Priest Rapids Dam. Yakima County was our home territory, our closest relatives lived there, and the house of my mother, Doris Campbell, in her orchard
on Route 1, Selah, Washington, was to be our base.

But on June 26, when the North Korean attack was described under black
headlines in the *Yakima Daily Republic*, we shelved the Columbia project,
expecting that I would be ordered momentarily to active duty. The *Republic*
and its sister the *Yakima Morning Herald* were owned by Colonel W. W.
Robertson, a colorful western newspaperman. Both were good papers; in
addition to readers in the town of Yakima, which in 1950 had a population of
less than 35,000, they were read widely up and down the Yakima Valley, keeping the county informed of national and international news.

On June 26, 27, and 28 the *Republic*, to which my mother subscribed,
carried one-inch front-page headlines that in turn announced "U.S. PLEDGES
ARMS TO SOUTH KOREA," "U.S. WILL DEFEND KOREA, FORMOSA," and "U.S.
IN KOREAN WAR." On each of these consecutive days the bold headings were
accompanied by descriptive and interpretive stories that on June 26 included
an opinion from Tokyo that if the United States "openly aids South Korea this
conceivably could lead to a shooting war with Russia," and through summer
and fall the paper continued to provide us with detailed war news.

On September 15, the headline proclaimed, "KNOCKOUT BLOW AIMED
AT ENEMY," in regard to our invasion at Inchon (see map) and elsewhere on
Korea's coasts that would push North Korean forces out of most of the South
Korean territory they had overrun. But then, on November 27, with Communist
China coming in on the side of North Korea and with China's massed infan-
try tearing holes in the UN advance, the *Republic* announced, "ALLIES FACE
MAJOR DISASTER IN KOREA."

Yet for all that, through months of one-inch black headlines, and now
with the war turning against us, from my perspective the prevailing attitude
in Yakima County seemed to be one of apathy. I was fourteen years old when
the Japanese attacked Pearl Harbor on the December 7, 1941, old enough that

even now, sixty-eight years afterward, I remember vividly reactions to that event as they were expressed in the Pacific Northwest. Overnight much of the citizenry, as well as military and naval forces, had prepared for war. Recruiting stations were swamped; lawyers, teachers, and doctors schemed to take leave from their jobs; housewives volunteered as farmhands and secretaries; and with their boats armed with deer rifles and searchlights, members of the Seattle Yacht Club ran night patrols of the islands and coves of Puget Sound.

Propelled by fear of an eminent Japanese invasion, shipbuilding and ship repair installations operated twenty-four hours a day, and the Bremerton (Washington) Navy Yard expanded exponentially. The army dug machine gun emplacements among the dunes of a boys' summer camp on the Long Beach Peninsula just north of the mouth of the Columbia River, and soldiers were posted around the clock on highway and railroad bridges, including railroad bridges in Yakima and other counties lying across the mountains in eastern Washington.

As I have described elsewhere, soon after Pearl Harbor, an American artillery captain drove through Yakima County, looking for a stretch of land in which "the biggest field guns in the U.S. arsenal could be fired in any direction without killing anything bigger than a coyote" (Campbell 1997, xii). Thus was created an artillery training center whose western perimeter lay four miles across the Yakima River from our orchard, and whose big guns were to rattle our windows and crack our cisterns for the duration of the war.

The fear of a Japanese invasion derived from a few facts and an abundance of rumors. One story had it that a Japanese pilot shot down over Pearl Harbor was found to be wearing a Hood River, Oregon, high school letterman's sweater, a story that has yet to be confirmed. The Yakima municipal airport was lengthened to accommodate three B-24 bombers. Each morning the bombers would fly over the Cascades, presumably to search the ocean for Japanese warships. A story soon circulated up and down the valley that on a recent evening one of the returning B-24s had carried one dead and two wounded crew members—again, a story that remains undocumented.

It was true, however, that soon after Pearl Harbor a Japanese submarine commander surfaced his boat just beyond the breakers, and with his deck gun lobbed shells into the environs of the little Oregon coastal town of Seaside. A quixotic act of class and derring-do, it bagged him only Douglas firs but nevertheless lent credence to the rumors.

Among other actual events that fed our fear was the Japanese invasion of the Aleutian Islands in the first week of June 1942, six months after Pearl Harbor. As ultimately unsuccessful as this occupation of the U.S. mainland territory turned out to be, to the press and many Americans it presaged an attack on the Northwest Coast. Worst of all was the perceived danger posed by thousands of Japanese-Americans living on or near the Coast, a nasty divisive rumor that prompted President Franklin D. Roosevelt's order to uproot more than 110,000 of these particular Americans and pack them off to relocation camps in the interior.

Because of these facts and rumors, and others like them, in the months following America's involvement in the Second World War the Pacific Northwest, including Yakima County, became an armed and ready camp, "on a full war footing" as the army and navy would call it.

But not in 1950, not in this Korean War, which in its beginning was described by President Harry Truman as a "police action," but which would result in more than 60,000 American casualties. Still, in the minds of those millions of U.S. citizens who had endured the early and middle 1940s, it was the Second World War that was *the* war, the *real* war. For one thing, the security of U.S. territorial boundaries was not in the least threatened by the Korean conflict. For another, on June 25, 1950, when North Korea attacked across the 38th parallel, not one American in hundreds had the foggiest idea of just where on earth Korea was supposed to be. Yakima County went on about its business with a sort of malaise, which as time passed was for me reflected in not hearing anything at all from the air force. Sue and I revived our Columbia River archaeological project, and with weekly calls to Mrs. Campbell's orchard from a telephone twenty miles up a dirt road, by fall we had finished the survey. Also during this time, through a correspondence course, I had learned barely enough German to qualify for a BA. (I had not graduated with Sue that spring because of my having failed to complete a foreign language requirement.)

We pitched a canvas wall tent in a grove of trees near an old log cabin whose gun ports stood witness to the final days of the Yakima Indian wars, and beside which ran a little creek that held some big rainbow trout. From that delightful camp we got to the outer parts of our search area with the help of two saddle horses borrowed from Sue's brother, Garretson Horsley, a Yakima Valley rancher, and we reached Priest Rapids' rocky islands in a small boat owned and commanded by Tom "River Rat" Stockdale, who was by acclamation the mayor of the upriver hamlet of Vantage Ferry. Back at Route 1, Selah, there were still no orders from the air force.

Professor Erna Gunther was chairman (not "chair" as in today's lingo) of anthropology at the University of Washington. She was a remarkable, dynamic scholar who, behind her back—with no reflection on Doris Campbell—I called my "Great White Mother." Professor W. W. (Nibs) Hill, an old friend of hers, was chairman of anthropology at the University of New Mexico, and with my beseeching she persuaded him to take me on as a *provisional* student in New Mexico's MA program despite my overall mediocre record at the University of Washington.

Consequently, still with no word from the air force, in October 1950 Sue and I moved to Albuquerque, where I enrolled for the academic year 1950–51, and Sue supported us by clerking in a downtown store. Then, in the summer of 1951, we joined the UNM archaeological field school in the hills of Lincoln County, New Mexico, where under Professor Paul Reiter I served as a graduate student foreman and Sue was paid to oversee the food requisitions and the assigning of cooking and KP duties to the twenty-odd student enrollees.

These adventures in New Mexico, for both familial and possible official reasons, required frequent telephone communications with the Campbell orchard, but by late July and the end of field school, thirteen months after the war's beginning, I was convinced that Korea had passed me by. This misconception was corrected by my brother Don, home on summer vacation from college, who called to say that he had signed my name for a registered government letter and asking in all innocence if I wanted him to open it and read it to me.

Frankly, the news was a welcome surprise; for once in my college career I had made rather consistently good grades. I was no longer a provisional grad student, both Sue and I needed a break, and for this new adventure the air force would pick up the tab.

The letter, dated "6 August 1951," began with "Subject: Orders into Active Military Service." Still, it was another six weeks before I was actually in the air force. There was a physical exam at a downtown military dispensary in Portland, Oregon, a week after which I was mailed orders announcing that I was physically qualified for active duty. Then there was time for a week of salmon fishing in British Columbia with Sue and brother Don, and finally, well into September, orders to report to a junior officer's assignment squadron at Lackland Air Force Base in San Antonio, Texas.[2]

The squadron's purpose was sending air force second lieutenants—most of them new graduates of ROTC or Officer Candidate School (OCS) programs—to permanent duty stations at air force installations scattered around the country and around the world. We were never to learn the magical process by which we were picked for duty in California, Germany, Greenland, or wherever, with the consequence that life in the assignment squadron had an air of mystery about it. The routine required that five days a week we reported for duty to squadron headquarters at 0800 hours, where as a substitute for roll call we signed in as present and accounted for, and looked for our names on a bulletin board tacked to a nearby wall. If we were there, we then asked the desk sergeant for orders to our new duty stations, but if our names were not posted we had the rest of the day off.

Finding your name on the board was like drawing a card in a poker hand; until the moment you read your orders you would know nothing about where you were headed, and the waiting and wondering ensured a 100 percent attendance at the daily signing in. As the days passed, our numbers were augmented by new arrivals while at the same time most of us were leaving on our permanent assignments, a balancing that kept our resident population to two or three dozen second lieutenants.

For us newly arriving recent ROTC graduates, our first and most immediate requirements were those of acquiring identification cards, finding housing, and getting into uniforms. An on-base office provided the ID cards, but we were told that the Lackland BOQ (Bachelor Officers Quarters) was full to capacity and that it was up to us to find our own digs, with the result that we were soon scattered around San Antonio in weekly-rate motels. As for the uniforms, the first sergeant unofficially advised us to see an avuncular Jewish tailor in downtown San Antonio. Having been in business since before the United States had entered the Second World War, the tailor told us that he had long since given up counting how many thousands of officers he had fitted (there were five military bases in San Antonio). He and his staff were experts, and in a few days he had us coming through Lackland's main gate looking like genuine second lieutenants.

Our slack time, including Saturdays and Sundays, allowed for our seeing the wonders of San Antonio—whose chief attraction of course was the Alamo— and spending hours on base in the Officers' Club where the drinks were cheap and where I learned the rudiments of chess and took up reading science fiction. I acquired this latter hobby when one of the club's patrons persuaded me to read Robert Heinlein's newly published *The Puppet Masters* (Heinlein 1951), which was to become a classic of its kind and which got me reading little beside science fiction until my interest waned six months afterward.

Besides these domestic pastimes there was for me the chaparral. San Antonio stands on ground that nearly imperceptibly slopes down to the Gulf of Mexico, whose nearest shore lies 150 miles southeast of the city. In a drier climate this landscape between San Antonio and the Gulf would be a grassy prairie or savanna, and if drier still it would be a desert. But as it is, rainfall is enough to have created a dense, low wood, more a thicket than a forest, which in Texas is called by the Spanish name *chaparral*.

We were told that these dense woods explained why the propeller-driven airplanes at neighboring Randolph Field—a training base for air force pilots— were painted a bright yellow, the better to find them when every once in a while one of them would plunk down in the chaparral. Chaparral was new to me. As a small boy, encouraged by my father with his bird dogs and trout rods, I had developed an abiding interest in natural history. Now, on the long weekends beginning Friday morning after roll call, and after looking in vain for my name on the bulletin board, I would drive south through the low woods

on back roads past little towns, in search of strange birds, javelinas, and alligators. I was especially interested in the alligators, which except for those that
were kept in the big fountain pool on El Paso's plaza (until one of them ate a
visiting lady's little dog) I had never seen. So between chess and science fiction and looking for alligators, duty at Lackland was a happy introduction to
the air force.

At the official level, this languorous routine was interrupted briefly by several days of physical and mental exams on base at Lackland. For the exams, my
fellow lieutenants and I were called up one at a time. The physical was more
or less standard except that for me it was more detailed than the one I had
taken at the dispensary in Portland, and that it paid extraordinary attention to
how well I could see.

The mental tests, canted more toward psychology than general knowledge or IQ, were administered by a captain. He began by having me spend
three hours writing an essay on my boyhood experiences and feelings, in
which I said that while in general I had had little to complain about, as a
skinny teenager in a high school of strapping Swedish American farm boys—
Johnsons, Swansons, Matsons, and Bjorks to name a few—I had been shut
out of playing varsity sports.

After I had handed him the essay, the captain gave me a series of fascinating questions relating to how a second lieutenant should or would react
to a variety of military situations. For example, and to paraphrase: "You are
an infantry lieutenant in a war zone. Your company commander gives you
an urgent handwritten message which you are to deliver by jeep to the commander of an adjacent company, and he tells you that under no circumstances
are you to tarry along the way. But before you reach the adjacent company's
command post you find in the road ahead of you an overturned jeep beside
which lies a soldier who, having failed to negotiate a curve is bleeding pro-
fusely from a leg injury. What do you do?"

After four days of this physical and psychological testing, I was offered
my choice of being assigned to flight school or to a scholarly year at the Army
Language School in Monterey, California, both of which I turned down because
they required my signing on with the air force for another four years.

Following the tests, I was ordered to oversee a Pullman car of thirty air
force buck privates who, having graduated from basic training at southern
bases, were on their way to duty at Fairchild Air Force Base near Spokane,
Washington. In my brief air force career, this was to be the first of a total of
two instances in which I commanded more than pencils and paper. It was
up to me, helped by a cheerful, capable corporal, to get the eighteen- and
nineteen-year-old privates to Fairchild AFB, a week's journey by rail. For

30 CHAPTER ONE

me, the journey would take ten days, counting processing the paperwork at Fairchild and flying back.

Typically, our names would come up on the bulletin board within two or three weeks of our arrival at Lackland, but in my case waiting for a duty station stretched on for two months. In retrospect my assignment to the thirty new airmen on their way to Fairchild implied that the air force had reason to keep me on hold.

We started from San Antonio on the Missouri, Kansas, and Texas Railroad— the MKT, but known most commonly as the "Katy." As it happened, half a dozen of my airmen were "colored," a term that, other than distinguishing blacks from whites, meant very little to a second lieutenant from the Pacific Northwest. But at the Katy station I saw with amazement and indignation that the lunch counter was sectioned off, one part being reserved for the "col-oreds," a condition about which I demanded to see the stationmaster.

When I was small, I had developed a special liking for stationmasters. These invariably portly, middle-aged men wore dark suits and vests and each kept a big gold watch tucked into a vest pocket, the watch connected to a gold chain draped across an ample belly. Upon the imminent arrival or departure of a train in, say, Yakima, Seattle, Spokane, or Billings, the stationmaster would stand in the middle of the passenger waiting room, take out his gold watch, open its lid, and in a loud, carrying voice announce the train.

Now, in the Katy station, here came the stationmaster, who in his dark suit, with the gold chain stretched across his belly, was identical to those I had known as a boy except that he had a Texas accent.

"Sir," I said, drawing myself up and trying to appear as impressive as the stationmaster, "I am Lieutenant John Campbell." Then I pointed at the lunch counter and said, "I object to some of my men being treated like this." The stationmaster nodded sympathetically and allowed as how it was a shame that "your colored soldiers" had to wait in a separate line, but this was the custom in Texas and there was nothing he could do about it. I argued futilely for another few minutes but the old boy stood firm and my airmen ate in their respective designated sections of the lunch counter. The "colored soldiers" made no complaint, understanding far better than I the rules of the South. But I could tell that they appreciated my attitude.

Then at long last there was my name on the board, together with those of second lieutenants Angelo Hillis and Nicholas Macrides, with orders to report to the CO (Commanding Officer) of the "581st Air Resupply and Comm. Wg, Mountain Home AFB, Mountain Home, Idaho [on] 21 Nov 51." That was all, and among our squadron officers, only one, a captain, had ever heard of Mountain Home AFB. He was a "retread"—a veteran of the Second World War—as was every officer we were to meet of the rank of captain or above, and he said that in World War II Mountain Home had been a U.S. Army Air Forces bomber base, but that as far as he knew it had long since been closed down. Further, he said that he had never heard of any such thing as an "Air Resupply and Comm. Wing." That was all we were to know about Mountain Home AFB or the 581st until we reported there for duty on the 21st of November.

Upon our arrival we joined a cadre of a few dozen officers, most of whom were second lieutenants (there was one captain and several first lieutenants, three of whom, and the captain, wore pilot or navigator wings) who with the same cryptic orders as ours were reporting in from around the country. As we reported to the 581st headquarters we were told that "Air Resupply and Communications Wing" was a cover name for an air force enterprise in psychological warfare about which we were to keep our mouths shut. Because I had imagined that Air Resupply and Communications had to do with loading and unloading airplanes, this revelation, whatever it might mean, was good news.

In the seventeen months that had elapsed between the outbreak of the Korean War and our arrival at Mountain Home, the air force had embarked on a clandestine psychological warfare venture that had its genesis in the Second World War. In that conflict the U.S. military had come to appreciate not only the value of psychological warfare, or "psywar" as it was to be called, but began to use it in conjunction with conventional military planning. Soon afterward we had become involved in a new, different war, one thrust upon us by Joseph Stalin's obsessive ambition to spread communism well beyond his country's borders. In answer to that threat, in 1947 the U.S. Army Air Forces, and Navy began creating programs designed specifically for psychological warfare. The Air Force Psychological Warfare Division Headquarters in Washington, DC, handled the planning, evaluation, and coordination of these efforts within the air force. Their plan called for the creation of "special operations wings," three of which were activated in 1951 and 1952 under the collective cover name of Air Resupply and Communications Service (ARCS), and the Military Air Transport Service (MATS) was given the mission of organizing, equipping, and training them (Haas 1997).

In the Second World War, General Eisenhower saw psychological warfare as a "specific and effective weapon" but on the whole regular military and civilian leaders viewed it as somewhat unethical and its chief tool, propaganda, as offending good taste. Still, the successes achieved by General Henry "Hap" Arnold and William J. "Wild Bill" Donovan in combined military and civilian covert operations during the Second World War encouraged the formation of these self-contained special operations units to meet the new threats that, with the heating up of the cold war, faced the United States.

Now in 1951, many of the guidelines the air force was using to plan allotments of personnel and equipment for its psychological warfare wings were a result of General H. H. Arnold's foresight. General Arnold, one of the first five-star generals in the U.S. military and a decorated veteran of both world wars, understood that the national security of the United States was dependent on the research and development of advanced technology. As one of the founders of the RAND Corporation, General Arnold urged his scientists to "think twenty years ahead." Since 1948, the RAND Social Science Division had conducted research on psychological warfare. Information provided by the RAND Social Science Division and the Air Force Human Resource Research Institute (HRRI), initiated in 1949 and run by the Air University at Maxwell Air Force Base in Montgomery, Alabama, gave the air force a strong theoretical basis for planning their psychological warfare program. The scheme as envisioned would be to get psychological warfare reduced to a formula that when applied through the new ARCS wings would bring the success that the air commandos had achieved in the Second World War.

William J. Donovan, who had distinguished himself in the military during World War I (receiving the Medal of Honor—among other awards—as well as the nickname "Wild Bill"), returned to service during the Second World War as a civilian, at the request of the president. As the creator and leader of the Office of Strategic Services (OSS), Donovan organized and administered its complex paramilitary operations with which Allied forces were able to weaken German strongholds in occupied Europe before the invasion of Normandy and to erode German strength after the invasion by supporting partisans and inserting agents engaged with espionage, intelligence gathering, and counter-intelligence (propaganda).

Donovan's teams, composed of military and civilian agents, covered objectives from Norway to France with a few going on to later OSS missions in China. Those composite forces were successful because of their ability to take the enemy by surprise. A big part of that surprise came from a quick tactical response to enemy encounters with little or no command overburden or protocol. Money, equipment, and personnel were arranged by direct order of the U.S. president to Mr. Donovan.

In the China-Burma-India theater, the operations of General "Hap" Arnold's air commandos and OSS units assigned to reinforce British troops in India were run the same way. Their efforts near the end of the Second World War prevented the Japanese from making serious incursions into India and China from Burma, and allowed regular U.S. military forces to concentrate pressure on the main Japanese forces in the Pacific Islands and move on toward the anticipated invasion of Japan.

The OSS was abolished in 1945, but when the Central Intelligence Agency (CIA) was created under the National Security Act in 1947, its administrators returned to Donovan's OSS blueprint. In 1949, the CIA went to the Department of Defense to request military support similar to the type given to Donovan's efforts in the Second World War. The army had kept its propaganda specialists separated from its guerilla warfare operations. The air force plan called for combining propaganda and espionage people in each ARCS wing.

In 1950 and 1951 the concept of mixing propaganda specialists who would use radio broadcasts and leaflets with spies and saboteurs who would be infiltrating enemy forces and running covert operations was not only new to the air force, but was ambitious. Approximately one thousand personnel were required for each of the Air Resupply and Communications Service wings, and manning the wing squadrons called for specialists in aircraft maintenance (fixed-wing B-29 bombers and SA-16 amphibians as well as H-19A helicopters), language specialists, guerilla warfare specialists, leaflet production specialists, and—before the air force was through—high-altitude balloon launch specialists. The squadrons as well as the entire wing were designed to be fluid and flexible enough to adapt to work in any theater of operations. To the dismay of the army, the air force was given the assignment. (That one squadron, Holding and Briefing, in each ARCS wing was to be shared by the CIA had, we assume, something to do with this decision.)

The wings were designated the 580th, 581st, and 582nd. Typical of the three "composite" wings, the 581st—my home for most of the duration of the war—contained five other squadrons in addition to its Holding and Briefing Squadron. For the aims of this book, the most pertinent among them was the 581st Reproduction Squadron whose principal purposes were those of producing and disseminating propaganda messages.

The Air Resupply and Communications Service was activated in February 1951 and was given sixty days to get its first wing, the 580th, deployed in the wilds of Idaho. The flying side of the ARCS mission would be difficult enough, but when it came to finding officers to command, staff, and train the wings with nontraditional, even controversial psychological warfare approaches to both hot and cold wars, the difficulties multiplied. In finding these essential commanders the Psychological Warfare Division, Directorate of Plans Headquarters U.S. Air Force in Washington searched its ranks for senior officers with experience in special clandestine operations, and among those found and ordered to senior staff positions in ARCS, Colonel William O. Eareckson (to be succeeded by Colonel John R. Kane) and Colonel John K. Arnold Jr. were given command of the 580th and 581st, respectively.

At Mountain Home, the 580th was activated in April 1951, the 581st in July of that year; more than a year later the 582nd, commanded by Colonel Robert W. Fish, was activated in September 1952. Each wing would contain a total of about one thousand officers and enlisted men, and while they would train at Mountain Home, each was designed for eventual deployment to air force commands beyond the borders of the continental United States. (As it turned out, the 580th was to see duty in North Africa and the Mediterranean, the 581st in the Philippines and Korea, and the 582nd in England.)

In addition to the three ARCS wing commanders, there was Colonel Herbert S. Beeks, who as the first senior officer to set foot on what was to be the "new" Mountain Home Air Force Base would stay on to command its 1300th Air Base Wing. This wing was a relatively large and complex organization. By mid-July 1952 it had a grand total of more than 4,600 assigned personnel of whom, in rounded-off numbers, were 685 air force officers, 3,435 air force enlisted men, and 550 civilians. As concerned base welfare, Colonel Beeks was chief housekeeper. As such, he looked after the air police, the fire department, the commissary, the hospital, and all other base units having to do with the necessities of everyday life. But additionally he was a principal in founding and staffing the air force survival school at McCall, Idaho, established for the training of ARCS air crews, and his 1300th Air Base Wing ran the psychological warfare school, of which I will have more to say.

With few exceptions, I saw these Mountain Home top brass only at a distance, such as at the once-a-month Saturday morning parades. The outstanding exception was that of my frequent brief encounters with Colonel John R. "Killer" Kane. His name was known to thousands of past and present air force people, military historians, and others for his heroism in the Second World War, in which he had led the U.S. Army Air Forces' Ninety-eighth Bomb Group on a raid from North Africa to German-held oil refineries in Ploesti, Romania. For this he was awarded the Congressional Medal of Honor. Each day at Mountain Home he would sit by himself at breakfast in the Officers' Mess, a good-looking, middle-aged man with an incipient scowl on what I imagined to be a Presbyterian face. (He reminded me of the well-known John Foster Dulles, who was soon to be U.S. secretary of state and who was said in the news to have a Presbyterian face.)

The story at Mountain Home was that although Killer Kane was a combat hero all right, he had lost so many planes over Ploesti that the army air forces, while giving him a Congressional Medal of Honor, told him at the same time that he would never be promoted to brigadier general, a decree that had left him in a poor frame of mind. Whether or not the story was true, his was an intimidating presence. As I passed his table each morning at breakfast, I would

say, "Good morning, Colonel Kane." He would reply, "Good morning, lieutenant," and I would go on my way. That was the total extent of any conversation
I ever had with him, but over the years it has permitted me to truthfully say,
"Oh, yes, I knew Killer Kane; at Mountain Home I used to talk with him every
morning at breakfast."

Via a narrow asphalt road, the base lay ten miles south of its namesake,
the exceedingly small town of Mountain Home, which stood beside the track
of the Northern Pacific Railroad. Both were sited on a flat plain, a northern
reach of the Great Basin Desert (Campbell 1997), dominated by the low-
growing, battleship-gray big sage known in the West as sagebrush. It is a
desert that seemed to stretch interminably in every direction, and that in
fact in one or another guise stretches southward to and beyond the Mexican
border eight hundred miles away.

We never learned how the town got its name. The nearest topographical
feature that might pass for a mountain is a range of hills running east and west
across the northern horizon. One would suspect that in the early days—the
Northern Pacific track was laid in 1883, and shortly afterward Mountain Home
was founded as a shipping point for lambs and wool—the town was named
with an eye for profit by either the railroad or land speculators, but Mountain
Home has no mountains.

By sheer coincidence, because of the stories I had heard from my father
and his brother George, I was one of the few men if not the only man on
base who knew something of the early history of the town and its surroundings. In 1906, the Campbell brothers, taking leave from Maryville College in
east Tennessee, had gotten off the train in Mountain Home with the idea of
becoming cowboys. Instead they spent a pedestrian year herding sheep. Forty-
five years later, except for the advent of gasoline-powered vehicles, Mountain
Home remained much the same as it had been described to me by my father
and uncle. Its only exports were still lambs and wool, and its First Street,
whose north side was occupied by the old stores, a restaurant, and two sheep-
herder saloons, still fronted on the Northern Pacific track.

Now, the job of rehabilitating the Second World War bomber base was
launched by Colonel Beeks, who, accompanied by thirteen officers and
twenty-four enlisted men, arrived in February 1951. As described in a base
report the following year, when Beeks and his cadre reached the derelict base,
"[t]heir eyes were greeted by a forlorn and discouraging prospect. Buildings
were roofless and floors were covered with piles of dirty snow. Litter was
strewn from one end of the field to the other. Weeds grew everywhere. There
were no mess facilities and meals had to be eaten in Mountain Home. There
was no fire-fighting equipment. Water pumps were operating, but leaky. Only

Control tower at Mountain Home Air Force Base 1951 (courtesy of Yancy D. Mailes, USAF)

one runway was useable. All of Colonel Beeks's personnel lived in permanent officers quarters, which were in a fair state of repair, until four barracks and a small mess hall could be patched up" (Air Resupply and Communications Association 2008).

In 1951 and 1952 I did not appreciate Colonel Beeks, but at this distance in time and after finding out more about him, he becomes the perfect choice for resurrecting Mountain Home AFB. He was an orderly, somewhat acerbic man who besides his other accomplishments attended to military behavior and protocol. In that first year, by the 18th of June he had established an obligatory, once-a-month Saturday Retreat Parade at which all officers and airmen not on other duty marched in squadron formation past the reviewing stand, upon which at attention and returning the salutes of our squadron COs stood Beeks and the ARCS wing commanders. And on Sunday, the 24th of that month, he announced the first religious service, conducted by the new base chaplain.

Very early on weekday mornings, Beeks would walk the two halls of the one-story rehabilitated ("rehabbed") BOQ, knocking on doors, making sure that the officers were up and on their way to breakfast. One morning he found second lieutenant Nick Macrides (one of the three of us who had been ordered to Mountain Home from Lackland) still in bed. For the next five duty days Nick and the colonel ate breakfast together. That was Colonel Beeks.

By the time of my arrival in November, the largely restored Mountain Home AFB had acquired its necessities, but it remained a picturesque survivor

Barracks at Mountain Home Air Force Base 1951 (courtesy of Yancy D. Mailes, USAF)

of the Second World War. With nearly all of its buildings rehabilitated prefabs, the base was of a kind that we young privates, corporals, and second lieutenants knew from the movies, while for many of the retreads—the sergeants, first lieutenants, captains, and higher ranks—it was a nostalgic relic.

Leaving out the romance, for arriving air force personnel and their accompanying dependents, neither the base, the town, nor its countryside offered much if anything in the way of good duty. Nearly all officers and airmen who lived on base were housed in the prefabs. Senior bachelor officers and married officers of senior rank with wives and children were domiciled in one of the few refurbished two-story buildings. Unmarried officers were afforded the dubious luxury of living on base in the rehabbed one-story BOQ; single enlisted men lived on base in rehabbed one-story barracks; and the rest of us, numerous enlisted and commissioned married couples for whom there was no room on base, rented what we could find in town or in Boise, the latter requiring a daily round trip of ninety miles. Sue and I—Sue having caught up with me at Lackland—lived in a cold-water trailer in Mountain Home.

Reflective of American demography, a sizeable majority of our newcomers were "Easterners" and most were city people. Few of us were from the rural West, and fewer still were from the western deserts. Boise, Idaho's capital, with a 1951 population of some 34,000, was the nearest big town of any kind. The nearest real cities, Salt Lake, Portland, and Seattle, were hundreds of miles away and effectively out of reach of Mountain Home. In other words, Mountain Home Air Force Base was in the middle of nowhere, and with the exception of the opinions of a notably small minority of outdoors-lovers, assessments of our social and natural landscapes ranged from poor to awful.

For that notably small minority of us who were outdoors people, being stuck at Mountain Home was like being Br'er Rabbit getting thrown into the briar patch. Sue and I, who belonged to this exclusive group, had grown up three hundred miles west of Mountain Home on the edge of this very same desert, and in that delightful summer of archaeological work on the Columbia River we had tented in the sagebrush. Then there were a few dozen shooters and anglers who belonged, who had brought along guns and tackle or who had sent home for them once we realized the virtues of the countryside. The East Fork of the Boise River, running down through the north-lying range of hills, was full of trout, and in fall and winter the canyon of the Snake River, the Columbia's largest tributary, was full of ducks. Trouting on the East Fork via a rough gravel road was a day's venture. But the Snake and its ducks were a thirty-minute drive south of the base, thereby allowing for early morning shooting before we reported for duty.

In the few days following our getting to Mountain Home I was involved in the usual housekeeping rigmarole that goes with arriving at or departing from a military base, and was at the same time given a variety of duty assignments. We, the members of the informal cadre of junior officers who had been ordered here with the same or similar cryptic orders, were naturally unaware of the growing pains being endured by the wing commanders and their staffs as they struggled to get the ARCS training programs—about which at that point we knew absolutely nothing—in operation. But we were bewildered by the part of their struggle that for more than a week had us shuffling from one to another unit. In turn, I was assigned to the 581st ARCS Wing and then to the 580th, and then again to the 581st.

My orders to the 580th directed me to Gowen Field, in Boise, where the 580th had an outpost, and where Sue and I then put a deposit on a two-room basement apartment. I reported for duty with the squadron, whose snorting bull logo I quote in the preface to this book. That duty held promise. I was told by the squadron adjutant that I was there to learn about secret kinds of operations that he would tell me more about later.[3] But after three days, and for reasons I will never know, I was ordered back to the 581st, in which I would dwell for the rest of my air force career. Now at Mountain Home, we new arrivals would begin our studies in Colonel Beeks's psychological warfare school, and would learn about the invisible line that bisected the ARCS domain.

Chapter Two

Mountain Home
and Georgetown

Base activities that related directly to psychological warfare were considered "classified," which meant secret or secretive to one or another degree—the official term "restricted" being the least secret among them—and were not to be talked about except among our peers. To encourage this secrecy the various units of the Mountain Home ARCS program were housed separately. We of Colonel Beeks's psychological warfare school were given our own small complex of prefabs that had been partitioned to provide classrooms and office space for our CO, a major, and his administrative staff.

As we reported for duty on the morning of our first day in the old buildings, we knew next to nothing about what we would be taught, nor about where in ARCS we would belong. After signing in and other preliminaries, we were told that we would be trained in propaganda and that our classwork would relate to essay writing and radio broadcasting. It was in this regard that we soon learned of the invisible line separating us from the rest of our on-base 581st (and 580th) colleagues, a line that reflected two major divisions of the practice of psychological warfare.

"Psywar" embraces a seemingly endless array of operations, most of which are secretive and are deployed both on the battlefield and behind or beyond enemy lines. They range from frontline radio broadcasting to supplying partisans with weapons, planting spies, and even arranging assassinations of enemy military or civilian bigwigs.

At one end of this spectrum, psychological warfare involves the use of propaganda composed of actual facts. During the Second World War this telling of the truth became known as *white* propaganda and its practitioners were called *white hats*, while *black* operations, with their *black-hat* practitioners, were based on outright lies or closely related deceptions. And at Mountain Home these two pronouncedly different approaches to waging psychological warfare were expressed by the invisible line, with us white hats on one side of it and the black hats on the other.

Ordinarily, there is so little glamour attached to white-hat activities that few historians care to write about them, though black-hat missions, fraught as they typically are with danger and intrigue, fascinate writers and readers alike, so that the resulting literature is abundant. The Second World War, especially its European theater, is a happy hunting ground for writers of black operations, some of them gruesome, some bloodless but bizarre, and most all of them fascinating.[1] In the Korean War, on a smaller scale, ARCS black operations covered many of the same activities as those of the Allies in World War II.

At our white-hat school we came to refer to black-hat territory as "the other side of the base," and it was made clear to us that whatever was happening on the other side was none of our business. As we would know eventually, what they were up to both in the air and on the ground was impressively realistic combat training. Even at Mountain Home, a long way from Korea and the Mediterranean, many of their operations were officially "Secret" or "Top Secret." Further, while most of us at the school were new to military life, a very large percentage of both their air crews and black-hat ground personnel were seasoned veterans of the Second World War.

As enumerated by Haas (1997, 79), the aircraft of both the 580th and 581st included, at Mountain Home, twelve specially modified B-29 four-engine heavy bombers, four C-119 twin-engine heavy transports, and four SA-16 twin-engine amphibians, all of which were hard to hide on the flat sagebrush prairie.

One would think that in their missions, the goings and comings of these noisy machines would be highly noticeable reminders of the presence of the two combat wings. But in fact, they practiced amazing stealth, a principal reason being that most frequently they were ordered out on long-distance night missions in all sorts of weather and over all sorts of terrain. The routes and purposes of such missions were known only to their crews and commanders, and of the three types of aircraft the only one we white hats ever saw at close range were the quite incredible B-29s, whose squadrons we filtered through on our way to the once-a-month review parade.

Accidents on both night and daylight missions ranged from the tragic crash of a B-29 in which all of its crew were killed, to an adventure of one of

B-29 specially modified heavy bomber on ramp at Mountain Home Air Force Base, 1952 (courtesy USAF)

the SA-16 amphibians that has come down to us as the story of "The Death Valley Albatross" (Koch 2007). The SA-16 was known as an Albatross because of its aquatic abilities. Close to sunset on January 24, 1952, with a crew of six, a 580th Albatross whose call name was *Zero-Zero-One* took off from a 10,000-foot runway at Mountain Home on an all-night navigational training flight. At an altitude of 10,000 feet and an air speed of 150 knots, the intention was to fly southwest for 750 miles to San Diego, where the plane would turn around without landing and fly back to base.

Given that the country over which they flew was mountainous desert and the least populated landscape in all the forty-eight states, this mission was typical of those demanded by the 580th and 581st brass. Their first checkpoint was Winnemucca, Nevada, a tiny cluster of lights in the sagebrush (about which its mayor in recent years has bragged that it is "a city of paved streets"). Their second checkpoint was Tonopah, Nevada, near the south end of the Great Basin Desert, and their third was supposed to be Barstow, California, square in the middle of the Mojave Desert. But not long after Tonopah, the number-one engine failed, and despite full power on number two, the plane, among looming mountains, began losing altitude at a rate of five hundred feet per minute, in response to which the pilot pressed the bailout button. As good luck would have it, the crew abandoned ship directly over the sandy floor of

SA-16 Albatross in hanger at Mountain Home Air Force Base, 1952 (courtesy USAF)

Death Valley, an ideal landing zone for the would-be parachutists in the middle
of the night.

With additional good luck the six of them touched down without a scratch
just fourteen miles over the uncluttered desert from the blinking lights of
Furnace Creek, the very small but famous Death Valley resort that is also occupied by a U.S. Park Service field headquarters. At Furnace Creek, following
their fourteen-mile walk under a starry sky, the crew told a cock-and-bull story
about why they were flying over Death Valley in the first place, and within
hours the Forty-second Air Rescue Squadron at March AFB near Sacramento
(who were also kept ignorant of the secret nature of the Albatross flight) sent
out a plane to pick them up on the Furnace Creek landing strip.

Meanwhile the Albatross, without its crew, flew on and on until it scraped
the top of a desert ridge, from which it slid down a forty-five-degree slope
until it came to rest in practically as good a condition as when it took off from
Mountain Home. And there it lies today, one of the least known wonders of
Death Valley National Park.[2]

In addition to the Air Resupply Squadron to which the Albatrosses belonged, the sequestered territory of each combat wing was occupied by a
Holding and Briefing Squadron, a Maintenance Squadron, an Air Materials
Assembly Squadron, a Communications Squadron, and a Reproduction Squadron. We were not to enquire about any of these six units, but as I will note, at
our psywar school we heard lectures from various of their members.

In that fall and early winter of 1951 only a select few of the officers and senior noncoms (noncommissioned officers) at Mountain Home knew the history of the air force effort that on short notice had resulted in the resurrection of the base and the creation and deployment of the ARCS wings. Unaware as we were of these accomplishments, we students did not appreciate the growing pains being suffered by Colonel Beeks's brand-new psywar school.

As envisioned in early 1951, the ARCS white-hat training plan contained three "stages" (Haas 1997). As I will describe further in this chapter, Stage 1 required that "carefully selected officers" would be ordered to four months of intensive academic background studies at Georgetown University in Washington, DC. Following this tour of duty, the Georgetown graduates were to enter training in Stage 2—Colonel Beeks's school at Mountain Home, which was known in the plan as "The Psychological Warfare and Intelligence School"—and which was intended to be split into Phase 1 and Phase 2. Over a span of several months, these two phases would offer courses in the specific characteristics and applications of military propaganda, including a course in "leaflet operations."

Stage 3, whose participants were a few outstanding graduates of the Georgetown and Mountain Home program, was reserved for volunteers only. Stage 3 called for further duty in a variety of government and academic environments, among them the Voice of America and the Specialized Warfare Course at Fort Benning, Georgia. Successful completion of the latter Stage 3 option would in effect convert its students from white-hat to black-hat careers.

On paper, the above outline reflected how we fledgling white hats were supposed to be trained, but on the ground that was not the way it worked. To begin with, and without our being told of the existence of the Georgetown program or of other of the plan details, we were ordered instead to Stage 2 at Mountain Home. Further, and more important, Colonel Beeks's school had no discernible resemblance to Stage 2 as described above.

Our classrooms were bare of practically all but blackboards. Maps were scarce; there were no slides or projectors. In our writing classes we were supplied with pens, pencils, and lined yellow pads for note-taking. Our essays were submitted in longhand or delivered orally for lack of typewriters. A microphone and a playback loudspeaker were all that we had for our work in radio broadcasting.

On balance, this scarcity of teaching aids was a minor problem. The main deficiency was the lack of qualified instructors. Except for black hats from the other side of the base who were, with one exception, only occasional visiting lecturers, no one in the school had anything but the most sketchy knowledge of psychological warfare. Accordingly, our regular teachers were chosen from our own student ranks. Because they knew nothing about psywar, they were charged with showing us how to write and how to speak in front of an audience.

This stopgap arrangement had one major fault. In becoming acquainted with our fellow classmates we learned that all of us were college graduates who had degrees in the arts and humanities rather than in engineering or the biological, earth, or natural sciences. Consequently, because of our majors in English, journalism, history, psychology, or whatever (mine was the only anthropology major), we had had plenty of practice at college in writing and in oral presentations. In other words, in these classes we would learn very little that we did not know already.

We were required to read mimeographed reports sent out by the Psychological Warfare Division, USAF Washington, which while less formal in format were similar to the "War Background" paperbacks published by the army during the Second World War. These handouts at Mountain Home presented up-to-date overviews of European and Asian countries, including Korea, and were appropriate to our prospective air force careers though they had no relationship to our day-to-day classwork.

A few useful additions to our ordinary classes included a short course on collecting propaganda data, taught by a visiting captain from black-hat territory across the base. He began by telling us that some 80 percent of the intelligence evidence necessary to the waging of propaganda warfare could be gathered from "open sources" such as newspapers and civilian radio broadcasts published or transmitted, in our case, in the United States, Canada, and Great Britain. Apropos of the urgency of the cold war, the class subject matter treated primarily Iron Curtain countries. In the class days we had with him, he demonstrated (from several different newspapers as an example) how by clipping items from disparate news stories we could piece together a picture of an event in Communist-dominated Romania, an event of a kind that the Romanian government was not inclined to advertise.

There were only occasional lectures by other experts, again from black-hat squadrons quartered across the invisible line. Lectures from these part-time teachers covered a number of fascinating subjects that did not relate directly to white-hat operations but were germane to a range of ARCS intelligence activities in which we might someday be involved (and in fact were involved before the war was over). Their subjects were map reading, geomorphology (characteristics of land surfaces), and survival techniques. One of these part-time teachers was a master sergeant, an old-timer who had been born and bred in the Great Smokey Mountains and was a genuine hillbilly. His explanations of wilderness living kept us on the edge of our seats, especially the many of us who were not outdoors people. Out of class we agreed that if the brass had let him, he would have taught us how to make moonshine.

An equally captivating visiting teacher was a black-hat captain, an Australian, who during the Second World War had somehow wound up as a second lieutenant in the U.S. Army. He taught us geomorphology, and was known on both sides of the base for his outdoor wisdom as well as for his peculiar experience in Germany in the Second World War. During the war's last months, he had been taken prisoner by a German infantry company. Soon after his capture, while they were getting ready to send him to the rear of the see-sawing line of battle, the German captain in command asked him if he might not arrange—under a flag of truce—to have the whole German company surrender to the Americans. This he did, with applause and a promotion to first lieutenant.

Even with these and a few other similar exceptions, our classwork was dull, though our teachers worked hard at their jobs and were treated by us with wry affection. Our favorite writing instructor, Second Lieutenant Finch—in whose class we delivered our presentations orally rather than on paper—was an enthusiastic teacher with a BA in English. For the course in radio broadcasting, First Lieutenant Chapman was both very good and the only teacher available who came anywhere near to having the right credentials. He had had no experience in broadcasting, but had majored in journalism. Because our regular course schedule offered no training in psywar, we were allowed wide latitude in the subjects we would write about or talk about. We chose and researched our own topics, which were read or heard by the teacher and class members. A day or two following our individual presentations, the teacher would give us his ungraded, confidential evaluations. This arrangement of letting us choose our own presentation topics resulted in my bringing to class a shotgun—most of the students had never seen a shotgun—and demonstrating the rudiments of wing shooting: pointing, swinging, and leading imaginary ducks. Lieutenant Finch's subsequent ungraded, encouraging evaluation read in part that "you overcame your nervousness early, stopped pacing and got your hands out of your pockets," and that "your steady pace, the repetition of key points, your illustrations, all pointed to well thought out preparation." He also liked my "high pitched twang . . ." Being an Easterner, he naturally thought I had a "twang."

Mine and most of the other presentations in that class were meant to be serious explications of topics we knew something about, but the more imaginative students among us provided extra entertainment. When Second Lieutenant Jack Allen's turn came (he was a solemn-looking recent graduate of officer candidate school), he got up and wrote on the blackboard that he was going to talk about the life and times of "Plugger van Dyke, the Little Boy Who Saved Holland." Another second lieutenant, whose name I do not recall, gave a similarly detailed talk in which he argued that in Belgium, at least, new babies were actually brought by storks.

In another class, the ordinary routine was broken one day when a captain we had never seen before barged in without knocking to read us a TWX (a teletype message) that had just arrived at 1300 Air Base Wing from Air Force Headquarters in Washington. The message put Mountain Home on Red Alert and advised us that incoming Soviet bombers had been intercepted and shot down that morning over New England. I remember vividly that while all of us believed this phony announcement, the four of our classmates who wore pilot or navigator wings were galvanized. One of them, and I quote him verbatim, stood up and shouted, "THIS IS IT!" There was pandemonium, and when in a few moments the truth was revealed, we booed the unknown captain out of the room.

Anyway, in spite of a few mitigating episodes such as Jack Allen's Plugger van Dyke and the counterfeit TWX from Washington, we were not much inspired with most of what we were getting at the school. Those of us who had had earlier experiences in the army or navy endured the routine with more grace than the new OCS and ROTC second lieutenants who had not seen previous service. But for all of us it was the sort of dull duty that generated a variety of low-level shenanigans which while they were irksome to our CO were not bad enough to get us into serious trouble.

The major who was our CO was unpopular among us for the main reason that he quite rightly insisted on our reporting for duty each weekday morning in correct military fashion. After lining us up for roll call and bringing us to attention, he would order "dress right dress!"—an order that often caused jostling and muttering on our part, and his yelling at us to "Shut up!"—and after returning us to attention we would shout "Here, Sir!" as he called off our names. John Attaway, one of my fellow second lieutenants with whom I would share future assignments, failed to show up one morning, and when the major demanded, "Where is Attaway?" we, standing at attention, answered in unison, "He went thataway." These and other similar roll call incidents were of a kind that discouraged our boss from being a friendly CO.

Across the base the black hats were up to their own minor misbehaviors. In chapter 1, I noted Colonel Beeks's obligatory once-a-month Saturday review parades. Dear as they were to the colonel, the parades were a bore to the 580th and 581st air crews, who beginning with their service in the Second World War had not cared for formality. On each appointed Saturday, before all squadrons on base reached the parade ground—Mountain Home's main runway—we assembled in front of one of the big surviving World War II hangers where we answered to roll call, and then straggled through two squadrons of parked B-29s to an open area beside the runway where we formed up for the parade. As we straggled through, we of the psywar school were awed by the

ARCS B-29s on ramp at Mountain Home Air Force Base, 1952 (courtesy USAF)

air crew members, who swung themselves up into certain of the B-29s whose bomb bays had been mysteriously left open.

These same air crews were responsible for the Big Red Mule, a shenanigan that surprisingly was either overlooked or ignored by Colonel Beeks. In the style of the bomber decorations of the Second World War, one of the crews had painted on the nose of its B-29 a big red mule with prominent, heart-shaped hooves accompanied in large letters by the name HOOF HEARTED: appropriate, and innocent too, until pronounced.

Looking back, Colonel Beeks's school had its virtues, including that our regular dull courses were useful reviews of our previous college work, and that from our mimeographed readings and visiting lecturers we were introduced to the nature of ARCS. But the school's most obvious virtue was its accommodation of elasticity. For various reasons we students would sometimes be ordered from the school on temporary duty assignments (TDY). In some instances this TDY was voluntary, as when a few of us were offered the chance to attend Squadron Officers School at Maxwell Air Force Base in Montgomery, Alabama. (This was a lengthy course of study in which we were told we would learn how to handle the paperwork and other matters essential to the operation of an air force squadron, a prospect that to me seemed considerably more dismal than the dull routine at Mountain Home.)

There were other TDY assignments that were not voluntary and that without prior warning would send us off base for weeks or months at a time. Whether these temporary tours were voluntary or not, we would leave school abruptly, in the middle of our coursework, then return just as suddenly later on. Meanwhile, in our absences the same or similar courses by the same or similar teachers were being taught over and over again, so that upon returning to base we would go back to our studies without in effect having missed a single class. Because of this advantage, in less than a year I attended Colonel Beeks's school on three different occasions.

The orders that took me from Colonel Beeks's school to Georgetown University were less opaque but still as unanticipated as those that had sent me from Lackland to Mountain Home. In part, they read that I was "placed on aprx fourteen (14) wks TDY to Georgetown Univ., Wash D.C. for the purpose of attending PW [Psychological Warfare] Sch. . . . reptg thereat NLT [No Later Than] 2 Jan 52." In separate orders, I was told more specifically to sign in at an address on Newark Street that turned out to be in a residential locality two miles or more from downtown Washington.

With Sue accompanying me, the journey east from Idaho was a drive through a cold, snow-covered landscape, during which we were extracted from a Wyoming drift by a snowplow whose two man-crew, with tourists in mind, carried a tow chain. Late on the night of the second of January we arrived at the address on Newark Street. It was a low, rambling building standing at the back of a wide lawn. Sitting at a small desk inside its front door, a man of few words in civilian clothes asked to see my ID and my orders, and told me to report the next morning to 1719 Massachusetts Avenue NW in the center of Washington. Other than that, he had nothing to tell me.

Thus began the "Georgetown Saga," as one of my former classmates likes to call those fourteen weeks: a semester of exceptionally hard work that reflected both imaginative thinking on the part of the air force and the intellectual reputation of the Society of Jesus. (Georgetown, the flagship of North American Roman Catholic schools, is Jesuit.)

A handsome brick Georgian building, 1719 Massachusetts Avenue NW was three blocks from Dupont Circle and two miles from the Georgetown campus. It looked as if it were a posh private club, but instead it housed the Institute of Languages and Linguistics, which was a part of Georgetown's School of Foreign Service. Its main floor was occupied by a classroom whose east wall was lined with a row of glassed cubicles in each of which sat a Georgetown student who on audiotape translated our teachers' lectures—in English—into foreign languages. (Except for the purpose of getting practice in translating, these students had nothing to do with us.) The remainder of this big room held two podiums and enough public-school-type desks for our air force psychological warfare class of three majors, fifteen captains, thirteen first lieutenants, and fifty-one second lieutenants.

The class was administered by two rather short, forceful men, the details of whose distinguished careers we were not to learn until years afterward. In 1952, when we knew Father Edmund A. Walsh, SJ, he was the vice president of Georgetown University and regent of its School of Foreign Service. Father Walsh, born in 1885, had founded this school in 1919 as the first of its kind in the United States. The U.S. State Department's own school of foreign service, whose reputation is on a par with Georgetown's, was established six years later. Among other accomplishments, he had served as a consultant and interrogator to the U.S. chief consul of the Nuremberg trials in 1946, and in Tokyo in 1948 he had served as an advisor to General MacArthur. His fame was such that at his death in 1956 President Eisenhower, in a detailed eulogy, remarked that Father Walsh "was a vigorous and inspiring champion of freedom for mankind and independence for nations . . . at every call to duty, all his energy of leadership and wisdom of counsel were devoted to the service of the United States" (NationMaster 2009). Father Walsh, with his monocle and mane of snow-white hair, was a demanding presence and a legendary critic of the Soviet system. One of his books, *Total Power*, was on our required reading list. As a member of an American relief organization he had known Russia firsthand in the early days of Bolshevik dominance, and his lectures were the most fascinating of those we would hear at Georgetown. To make a point, he would take off his monocle and wave it in the air, saying, "Now take this down the way I am telling it!"

Colonel Leon E. Dostert, U.S. Army, Retired, was the official director of our Georgetown program. Born in France in 1904, in 1949 he and Walsh had founded the Institute of Languages and Linguistics as part of the School of Foreign Service. Both before and following the Second World War, he pioneered language teaching programs and techniques in the United States and in European countries. And during that war he served first with the French army before being commissioned a major in the U.S. Army, where he became an aide to General Eisenhower.

For his wartime service he had received an impressive array of ribbons and medals that from the United States included, among others, the Legion of Merit with Oak Leaf Cluster and the Bronze Star with Oak Leaf Cluster. And from France he had been awarded, among others, the rank of Knight of the Legion of Honor and the Croix de Guerre with two Palms (MacDonald 1967). When we were his students we knew no more about his accomplishments than we knew about Walsh's illustrious career, but Dostert looked and acted like a colonel and he was addressed as such by everyone up and down the line, including Father Walsh.

Colonel Dostert was the engine who ran the class. In our first two days he explained what would be required of us, including that at school we would wear civilian clothes only. For the rest of the semester, each weekday morning at 8 AM sharp he informally brought us to order and introduced the teacher of the day by giving us a brief biographical sketch. He then turned us over to our most senior student major who would take roll, after which the morning's session would begin. Aside from this administrative work, Colonel Dostert's contributions to our classes were his own lectures, his learned introductions to our other teachers and their subject matter, and his summations of or addenda to what they were talking about.

An archetypal, voluble Frenchman, he continuously used his right hand for emphasis, and as a much admiring witness he provided color and insight to General Eisenhower's crusade in Europe. He was an ardent Anglophile. In his lectures he commonly referred to England and her Second World War history as "that tight leetle island" and to her people as being among the bravest of the brave.

Georgetown's School of Foreign Service had begun accepting air force officers for training in psychological warfare in the fall of 1949. In the fall of 1950 an accelerated fourteen-week course was added to the school's more lengthy psywar program and by June 1951 more than 220 officers had graduated from or were in training in these or closely related graduate courses (Johnson 1974). Our class of eighty-two students belonged in the accelerated program, a compressed semester of fourteen weeks.

The institute's teaching staff numbered ninety-four civilian faculty and associate faculty members for most of whom English, in today's parlance, was a "second language." Among them, they taught a total of more than thirty foreign languages, including a few so esoteric that few of us had ever heard of them. Some of these faculty gave courses in subjects other than languages and linguistics, among them anthropology, economics, human geography, history, political science, psychology, and sociology. And from them we were assigned our thirteen teachers who in addition to Dostert and Walsh included the notable émigrés Constantine Boldyreff, Vladimir Gsovski, and Majid Khadduri. Occasional visiting lecturers were other civilians and officers from the Pentagon.

In some cases doubling or taking turns, these teachers taught us eight courses: A Survey of Major World Cultures; Values at Stake in the Present Ideological Conflict [the cold war]; Political Structures and Practices; Mass Reactions in Psychological Warfare; Major Aspects of Contemporary U.S.

Foreign Policy; Psychological Warfare Techniques and Practices; Economic Practices in the Present World Situation; and Analyses of Current Developments in Relation to Psychological Warfare (Georgetown University 1952). Together, these classes added up to a daunting 260 "clock hours" of lectures. From 0800 hours until noon on all weekday mornings we sat together in the big room listening to the wisdom of these eminent scholars and taking stacks of notes.

We eighty-two students had come in from all over the country, and unlike our class at Mountain Home, which was composed of officers who had majored in the humanities, the Georgetown class reflected a wide range of academic backgrounds. Further, we soon learned that many of us at Georgetown had actually volunteered for duty in the Air Resupply and Communications Service instead of having been ordered to ARCS, as some of us had been without our prior knowledge or having had any say in the matter.

In the months following the creation of ARCS, and with an eye toward the recent successes of the Georgetown school, the air force had sent circulars to many or most of its bases, advertising discreetly the new program and inviting officers to apply. Apparently, transfer orders to successful applicants took precedence over whatever other duties they were performing at the time. Among my fellow students at Georgetown, when Second Lieutenant Charlie Grill, of the 581st, applied and was accepted he was assistant base adjutant at Luke AFB in Phoenix, Arizona, while Second Lieutenant Fred Brody of the 580th applied and was accepted upon his graduation from OCS at Lackland.

Somewhat surprisingly in view of the intensity of the lecturing, there was room for brief questions or other remarks from the class. I have mentioned that we represented a wide range of academic backgrounds, but for one student this background did not appear to be noticeably academic. He was an older, rough-hewn talkative major who in class insisted on calling the Soviet Union the "So-vite" Union, and who on class breaks entertained us with droll stories and short poems, one of the latter of which had to do with the Pentagon, which stood in nearby Virginia not far across the Potomac River from Georgetown.

No one at Georgetown seemed to know, or at least no one was telling us, very much about the Pentagon. Supposedly it was inhabited by high-ranking officers who were planners of top-secret military and naval operations, but who according to what we heard at school were accused by cynics of getting their plans by looking into crystal balls. During our semester at Georgetown, visiting lecturers included two Pentagon officers of uncertain rank who appeared in class in civilian clothes. Following their visit, old "So-vite Union" entertained us with:

Those planners are a funny bunch
They wear neither sword nor pistol
They walk bent over, never run
Because their balls are crystal.

Most of our courses were canted toward giving us overviews of the histo-ries and modern-day characteristics of primarily European and Near Eastern countries. These courses, with exceptions, had little directly to do with actually waging war, although all of them related to the cold war. In the case of Italy, as a typical example, we were taught in detail its political and economic demog-raphy, including governmental structure, industrial and agricultural productiv-ity, transportation systems, and the like.

The above-noted Vladimir Gsovski began by lecturing on "Marxism and Other Revolutionary Currents in Russia prior to 1917," an "introduction" that was anything but an encapsulated outline. Instead, it was composed of names, dates, and detailed descriptions of politics and revolts beginning with Alexander II, who became emperor in 1861. In his second series of lengthy lectures, again in great detail, Professor Gsovski told us about "The Origin of the Soviet System of Government," breaking it down into six parts: Form of Government—A Matter of Tactics; March 1917 Revolution; Petrograd Soviet; Soviet vs. Provisional Government; Bolsheviks on the Road to Power; and Soviet Government.

The two courses in psychological warfare differed in that the first, "Mass Reactions," was an historical account of the successes and failures of propa-ganda as it had been received by civilian populations, especially in the Second World War and in reference mainly to Europe, while the following course, "Psychological Warfare Techniques," brought us up to early 1952.

Among other subjects, this course dealt with what the U.S. government was doing at home in enlarging our global psywar efforts, with the Soviet anti-Western propaganda programs aimed at their own Russian citizens and those of other countries behind the Iron Curtain, with the current role of Voice of America broadcasts to these same populations, and with the battlefield psy-war techniques we were currently employing in Korea. Most important to my career were the lectures on preparing and delivering leaflets in the ongoing Korean war.

Apropos of these two courses, each of us was assigned fifteen semester hours of "Area Problems in Psychological Warfare." The aim of this course was to give us practice in devising a psywar program for a particular geographical or political region. For this purpose our eighty-two-member class was bro-ken into study groups of four or five students. Each group was responsible for a particular country or region chosen by Colonel Dostert. We were then turned loose as teams to track down the necessary library sources (the nearby Congressional Library was a much used convenience) and prepare a typed psywar plan to be handed in two weeks before the end of the term.

Over the years I had developed an academic (and romantic) interest in the Far North, an interest that had included a summer of placer mining in Alaska. That interest now prompted me to petition Colonel Dostert for permission to write a one-man seminar paper on the Arctic and Subarctic. On a standard School of Foreign Service Student Request form I wrote, "It is requested that 2nd Lt. John M. Campbell, Jr. be given permission to do [a psychological war-fare] area study among the circumpolar peoples . . . the reason for this request is two fold. 1. No known studies of this nature have been made in this area which the undersigned believes to be important in the psywar sphere. 2. The undersigned is personally interested in the problem."

Colonel Dostert sent it back with "Approved as Individual Study. D[ostert]" and I was on my way to writing an enthusiastic, if rather amateurish paper on the potential contributions of subpolar Natives in the event of a shooting war with the Soviets. In collecting data for this essay, I became acquainted with the illustrious Arctic expert Dr. Henry B. Collins Jr. of the Smithsonian Institution, a man who in future years would have much to do with my success as a gradu-ate student at another university. And because of the paper's unusual nature and my arguing over its potential future value after the Korean War, following my release from active duty in 1954 the air force kept me on as a captain in the Retired Reserve.

This classwork and the seminar paper were only part of the drill. Every day, including Saturday and Sunday, each of us was required to buy copies of the *New York Times* and the *Washington Post* from which we compiled scrap-books of clippings having to do with what we were learning at Georgetown; the bulging scrapbooks—most of us filled several of them—were due with our seminar reports. Finally, near the end of the semester and in front of the whole class, we were subjected individually to tough oral exams.

For each of the nine courses (counting the seminar), we were awarded grades of "unsatisfactory," "satisfactory," "very satisfactory," or "honors." At graduation we were given our diplomas and typical college transcripts listing our courses and testifying to our having earned twenty-one credit hours "in winter semester 1952." In a memorandum, Colonel Dostert laconically justified the quite incredible foreshortened semester by remarking that "the students enrolled in the course possessed undergraduate degrees and approximately one third of them held advanced degrees. The courses were conducted on a level which reflected that situation." Well, maybe so, but for most of us who survived that Jesuit-engineered academic psychological warfare term, it would go down as the most arduous semester in our past or future careers.

As a finale, Father Walsh and Colonel Dostert gave us a graduation party in a grand, oak-paneled room on the main Georgetown University campus at which we wore full dress uniforms and where with relevance to our membership in the secretive ARCS, we were told that that very morning Radio Moscow had congratulated each of us by name on our graduation from the Georgetown psywar school.

Chapter Three

The Voice of America
and Clark Field

From Georgetown we scattered to the four winds. We were not told where our classmates were being sent, but through the grapevine we heard that two or three had been ordered, ominously, to jump (parachute) school at Fort Benning, Georgia. Among the several of us returning to Mountain Home, three of my classmates and I had hardly unpacked when we were handed orders to the Voice of America headquarters in Manhattan. We were to report to Mr. James F. Thompson no later than "8 May" for 120 days of OJT (on-the-job training). As I noted in chapter 2, the ARCS training plan called for several successive psywar classes at Georgetown from which a few students would be selected for further training at the Voice of America. Because I was a "satisfactory" but hardly distinguished graduate of the Georgetown University program, the reason for my being selected for the VOA was puzzling, but still I was among the chosen few.

"*This is the Voice of America*" was the sign-on given by broadcasters working for the Office of War Information shortly after the United States entered the Second World War,[1] and after the war this greeting continued to be used as the Office of War Information was closed and the International Broadcasting System (IBS) radio programs were folded into the State Department. Voice of America programming was never heard in the United States, but its scripts were prepared here and by late 1949 its programming format was carefully controlled by the Office of International Information, which was parented by the State Department's Office of Public Affairs. In the years since its launch in

1942, the Voice has carried many different official titles. It has frequently been investigated and nearly extinguished by the U.S. Congress, which at one point favored passing it over to the United Nations. Yet it has kept its working name, the Voice of America, to this day.

In early 1950, broadcasts by the VOA seemed to cause as much concern, debate, and paranoia among members of the U.S. Congress as they did in the Soviet Cominform and Politbureau. In the spring of 1950 President Truman, the Department of Defense, the State Department, and the CIA were agreed that a hard-line anti-Communist, most particularly anti-Soviet, propaganda campaign would guide U.S. psychological warfare initiatives. Congress, however, was reluctant to fund the VOA. The anti-Communist sentiments of the legislative branch were tempered by its distrust of the growing power of the executive branch and by the fact that the VOA's success was difficult to measure in terms relative to dollars invested. In addition, some congressional representatives felt that the use of information obtained from partisans or spies and broadcast abroad by the United States was unethical, and that the use of propaganda was detrimental to our national image. Ironically, by sparking the Korean War, Stalin swung the support of the American public and thereby the U.S. Congress to any effort to prevent the spread of Soviet power. U.S. psychological warfare operations including broadcasts by the VOA (many of which were aimed straight at the Soviet Union) were allowed funding, and Truman's "Campaign of Truth" got under way. Despite Russian claims of innocence in the precipitation of the Korean War, not only did the Eighty-first Congress loosen purse strings after June 25, 1950, for Department of Defense budgets, which allowed the air force to field its first Air Resupply and Communication Service wings, it authorized funding that allowed the Voice of America to expand its broadcast activities at a rate not seen since the Second World War.

On February 12, 1950, Edward W. Barrett was appointed by the Truman administration to the position of Assistant Secretary of State for Public Affairs and thereby became the head of the Office of International Information of which the VOA was a large and controversial part. Barrett, a career journalist whose service with the Office of War Information during the Second World War had acquainted him with the VOA, came to the State Department after working four years as the editorial director of *Newsweek Magazine*. Foy Kohler, a career Foreign Service officer fluent in Russian and having most recently served in the American Embassy in Moscow, was appointed chief of the VOA. Not only did Kohler have the responsibility of managing the Manhattan Branch of the VOA, he oversaw engineering and transmitter construction crucial to the VOA's broadcast links as well as handled public relations for the Voice in the United States and abroad.

Earlier editorial guidelines that featured slick, advertisement-style copy of what happy Americans (enjoying the benefits of democracy) were up to in Iowa and Texas were replaced with carefully pointed, open news coverage of how things were working for people in Eastern Europe and the Soviet Union under Communist control. As the Soviets extended their reach into Southern Europe and continued pressure in Korea, the VOA doubled its staff. Budget allocations of 13 million dollars for 1951 and the promise of 21 million by 1952, however, came with strings attached: additional congressional oversight. Almost overnight, the Voice of America developed an insatiable appetite for translators, writers, and analysts. Scripts vetted for accuracy and best regional impact also had to be translated into an exponentially growing number of languages understandable from Budapest to Damascus, Leningrad to Lebanon, and Istanbul to Beijing. They also had to be available to any and every member of the U.S. Congress. Assistant Secretary Barrett likened this task to keeping a 531-member board of directors satisfied. With broadcasts of any form, including music as well as news, being scrutinized by multiple levels of the State Department as well as by Congress, the VOA was not a fast-breaking-news service. Still, VOA listeners who were receiving little, if any, information on the public works and politics of their own governments were hungry for news, even late news. As an increasing number of people behind the Iron Curtain tuned in, the Kremlin spent more time and money jamming radio transmissions. Barrett pictured VOA broadcasts for congressional budget-hawks as fleas whose purpose was to keep the Russian Bear so busy scratching it had no time to molest others. By debunking Russian propaganda and depleting the Soviet treasury, the VOA was an effective weapon of psychological warfare and, as both Barrett and Kohler were quick to point out, an excellent investment of U.S. tax dollars.

Voice of America headquarters occupied floors in the General Motors Building on West 57th Street near the west end of Central Park, where on the appointed 8th of May we four from Mountain Home were joined by seventeen other air force junior and field-grade officers arriving from air force units across the country. Mr. Thompson, as his "Mr." implied, was a civilian, as were all other resident VOA personnel, to our knowledge. His title was Chief, Division of Radio Operations. Following three days of informal orientation lectures, Thompson gave each of us a memorandum directing us individually to various offices on the VOA floors "for such duties, commensurate with his rank and position as may be assigned." Three other lieutenants and I were sent to the office of "Chief, Operations Intelligence, IRP [Division of Radio Programs]."

Among the memo's several paragraphs—which applied mainly to our assignments and to administrative matters—two of them reminded us that whatever our on-the-job training might be, we were to take it seriously.

Paragraph 3 said that "these officers are to be assigned full time duties as rapidly as they become indoctrinated. They should be fitted into the respective units, and may be assigned any shifts worked or duties performed by the unit by [civilian] personnel of a comparable grade."

Paragraph 4 said, "Each supervisor, to which an officer is assigned, will be expected to furnish comments on the capabilities, progress and interest of each assigned officer at the end of the first 30 days of duty and at the end of the tour of duty." Paragraph 6 announced that "[t]hese officers will wear civilian clothes while on duty with IBS."

In his early forties, Mr. Foy Kohler had served as U.S. charge d'affairs in Moscow and was one of the foremost authorities on the Soviet Union. In 1966 he was to become President Kennedy's ambassador to the Soviet Union, where his understanding of the mindset and ploys of Soviet leaders proved crucial in resolving the Cuban missile crisis (Kohart 2001). At the VOA in 1952, he had a manner about him that befitted his past and future career. We saw him at obligatory weekly meetings held for the VOA professional staff where in precise, authoritative lectures, which allowed for few if any comments or questions, he reviewed the accomplishments and shortcomings of the past week's effort, and urged further diligence on our part. Hopefully he had another less austere side to him, but if he did we never saw it because we on-the-job trainees only knew him from the backseats of the big, tiered briefing room.

Sue and I had taken a small apartment over a French restaurant a few blocks from General Motors, from which I walked to work in the offices of Mr. John Pauker, whose title at Operations Intelligence was Policy Guidance Officer. John Pauker, our boss and mentor, came across as a different kind of man, although naturally the four of us who worked in his domain got to know him at much closer range. A product of Fieldston and Yale, Pauker had served with the Office of War Information, broadcasting from Algiers to Axis countries during World War II, and had joined the VOA after leaving the army. Born in Hungary and reared in New York, John was typical of many VOA commentators and analysts who served their adopted home (the United States) as well as their country of origin through broadcast news. In 1956 John Pauker went back to Hungary to cover the Hungarian Revolt as a commentator for the VOA. In addition to being an established poet and an enthusiastic teacher, he would become the chief policy guidance officer for the United States Information Agency of which the VOA was the largest element (*New York Times* 1991). We began our four months under Pauker's tutelage with his introducing us to the contents of diplomatic pouches. Locked and sealed in accordance with international protocol, the pouches had reached Washington from U.S. State Department personnel posted to the USSR and their Eastern European satellites.

As was the case at Georgetown, our education at the VOA had little to do directly with Korea. Pauker's job, or rather that part of it pertaining to visiting psywar officers, was teaching us VOA broadcasting as it was aimed not exclusively but most particularly to those European countries lying behind the Iron Curtain. In 1952, the cold war had become as dangerous as it would ever get, which explained why our training at the VOA and Georgetown had so much to do with Europe. The uneasy feeling that the war in Korea was part of Stalin's strategy to pull American arms, manpower, and money away from Europe, and the creation of the North Atlantic Treaty Organization (NATO), took precedence in upper-level decision making by the Joint Chiefs and the National Security Council even at the height of the Korean War.

Perhaps some or much of what the pouches had to say had been removed by U.S. officialdom before they got to John Pauker. Be that as it may, in our first two weeks he lectured informally on the propaganda aims of his office and explained the sorts of events reported back to us from Communist Europe that the VOA could best exploit. He also had us searching the reports for story lines that to our minds, without his prompting, would appeal to our prospective audiences, and he accepted or rejected our choices according to their potential appeal to specific groups, including soldiers and sailors.

It was a fascinating game, based on the fact that most of our audiences had not been privy to the news we got from the pouches and that dire punishments to the contrary, there were thousands of radio receiving sets hidden behind the Curtain. Pauker turned down many of our choices for various reasons, including that they did not fit our aims, did not appeal to an appropriate audience, or sometimes smacked of being phony. Then, as he looked over our shoulders he put us to writing practice copy, and at the end of those first weeks we were writing the real thing—actual radio messages to the Soviets and their allies. All of our work in Pauker's office was white hat, using open news without polemic to weaken the enemy and bolster support for America. Our compositions had only to do with radio broadcasting, harking back to our cobbled-together training at Mountain Home. In both instances they were required to be pithy, to the point, and short, qualities that lent themselves equally to both radio and leaflet writing. In our brief messages, which ordinarily amounted to no more than three or four minutes per broadcast, we repeated verbatim or in summary what our printed sources had to say and then added a few editorial comments. Some of our short, short stories stood up well without the help of commentary. From early on in its history the USSR hierarchy (and later those of its satellites) had expressed a remarkable attitude concerning what citizens should or should not be told about internal misfortunes. Because of this peculiar paranoia, domestic catastrophes such as major train wrecks and air crashes were kept secret, leaving friends and relatives wondering what had become of their loved ones. Very often, we knew what had become of them, and our factual descriptions of these events were all that were needed to get our message across.

The VOA coverage of Oksana Kasenkina's leap to freedom in the summer of 1948 proved how powerful a straightforward news broadcast could be. With no State Department protocols to hinder them on their home turf (New York City), VOA broadcast releases were not only nearly instantaneous, but were the essence of white-hat propaganda. Kasenkina jumped from the third floor of the Russian Consulate. A Russian schoolteacher, she had been allowed to travel to New York as a tutor for the children of Russian diplomats. She was to return to her Russian homeland after three years in America. Although she spoke no English and carried no secret messages, her decision to risk her life by leaping to freedom became a symbol of resistance to totalitarian regimes. The VOA relayed the news to the U.S. Embassy in Moscow within hours, and through their Iron Curtain stations quickly thereafter. Our embassy staff hit the streets of the Russian city and reported Soviet citizens discussing the event that same day. When the Kremlin finally released their version of the story over a week later, it was so convoluted that U.S. informants reported horse-laughs and open guffaws from the normally more guarded VOA listeners in the shops and markets of Moscow. Though Oksana Kasenkina's story would go on through political embellishments and spin—her survival, her testimony on the miseries of Russian women, her trial, and the U.S. presidential grant of amnesty—it was her jump that gave the VOA reporters all the news they needed and evidence that the Voice was being heard in the heart of the Soviet Union (Maeder 2000; Tyson 1983).

On a more modest level, one of our stories of a not atypical Soviet execution required only a one-line comment. One of our sources reported that within the past week a Muscovite had been shot in secret and without trial for stealing a pig. One of my air force office mates sent this one back to Mother Russia, adding only as its title, "Justice Kremlin Style."

John Pauker, as it happened, was great to know both in and out of "class." He was a quintessential New Yorker and proud of it. Within a week or so of the four of us having become his newest crop of air force pupils, he announced one day, "There are country rats and city rats, and I'm a city rat," going on to say that on lunch hours he would educate us rustics in where to eat in Manhattan. Afterward, with Pauker as tour guide, on our rather generous lunch hours we rode the subway to a succession of obscure yet extraordinarily good restaurants, beginning with a hole-in-the-wall Russian borscht place whose tables were covered with red and white checkered oilcloth.

Sue and I had seen little of New York before my VOA assignment so on our off-times we further explored the canyons of Manhattan among whose many wonders was the Café de France. By luck, John Wasson, one of my University of Washington pals, now a navy ensign, was on TDY with his wife, Jean, in New Jersey just across the Hudson River. The four of us, joined sometimes by my brother Don, a Yale senior who would come down from New Haven, made our social headquarters this marvelous little restaurant a few steps below the sidewalk at 313 West 46th Street, just west of 8th Avenue. Café de France was presided over by a slim, handsome Frenchwoman who, because she wore navy blue dresses with white collars, we called Mam'selle Hepzibah after the dainty little black and white skunk in Walt Kelly's *Pogo*. The comic strip *Pogo*, featuring the exploits of an Everglades possum and his friends, including Mam'selle Hepzibah, was the rage at that time of more or less liberal-minded college students and junior officers.

Mam'selle Hepzibah's four waitresses were pretty girls who had recently arrived from Brittany. Mam'selle herself had come over at the end of the Second World War during which, in her native France, she claimed to have developed a special affection for American officers as compared with German, French, British, and other countries' officers. Because of this esteem she occasionally kept us over after dinner and after the restaurant was closed for the night, when we would have drinks on the house and talk until the wee hours. The VOA was good duty indeed.

True to its secretive reputation and of course without our being told, the 581st had been ordered in July to Thirteenth Air Force headquarters at Clark Air Force Base on the Philippine island of Luzon, a move that would leave behind at Mountain Home about two dozen of us who at the time were off on a variety of TDY assignments. After the wing had gone off without us and we had returned to Mountain Home, we were assigned the same dull routine as before, now as orphans attending classes with junior officers of the 582nd. None of us was told, nor did we anticipate, that we would be catching up with the 581st in the Philippines. So, to escape further academic boredom I applied for a permanent transfer as an instructor to the Air Force Escape and Evasion School at McCall, Idaho. The job called for reasonable sophistication in how to get along in the out-of-doors and following an interview at the school, I was accepted. Alas, on December 22, three days after having been told they would take me and while the McCall officers were initiating the paperwork, we two dozen or so stragglers were ordered to Camp Stoneman, California, "for further assignment to Headquarters 13th AF." (The Thirteenth Air Force, rather than the Military Air Transport Service, MATS, was now home to the 581st.)[2]

Troop transport USNS *David C. Shanks*, 1953 (US Navy photo)

On February 10 we sailed from the Embarcadero in San Francisco Bay on a big gray troopship, the USNS *David C. Shanks*, named for a U.S. Army general. USNS stands for U.S. Naval Ship, but according to the long tradition of troopships her captain (a lieutenant commander) and crew were merchant mariners, not navy men.[3]

Four hundred and eighty-nine feet long, with a displacement of 10,418 tons, the *Shanks* had once been a passenger liner, as attested by her elegant hardwood decks and spacious cabins. In fact, from 1930 (the year she was launched) until 1943 (when during the Second World War she was turned over to the army), she plied the Atlantic between New York and London as the SS *American Farmer*, which carried passengers and cargo under the flag of the American Merchant Marine Lines (Naval Historical Center 2008).

Now, in 1953, her compartments were filled with more than one thousand troops. Soldiers, marines, and airmen as well as dozens of cabin-class officers, including several of the Philippine constabulary, traveled along with U.S. officers' wives with children on their way to join their husbands on the other side of the ocean. Getting from San Francisco to Manila Bay was an experience in smooth sailing under an expert skipper, yet smooth as it was, the crossing was roundabout. We stopped at Honolulu, an atoll in the Gilberts, Guam in the Marianas, and, after three weeks at sea, finally tied up at dockside in Manila Bay, some sixty overland miles from our destination, Clark Field.

For me the long voyage had its attractions. My interest in natural history was nourished by the incredible coral islands, flying fishes, and albatrosses—and as I noted in the margin of my copy of Blackman's *Birds of the Central Pacific Ocean*, by the red-footed booby that late in the afternoon of February 21 and six hundred miles east of Kwajalein flew in from the open sea to hitch a ride on the *Shanks*.

An attraction of a different kind that ensured I would not suffer from boredom in those three weeks was my *Shanks* military assignment. As we boarded the ship in San Francisco, several of us junior officer passengers were given shipboard duties. Mine was that of overseeing a troop passenger compartment that contained about 150 army and marine corps privates who slept in bunks stacked in tiers of five, and who during daylight hours were allowed the open air of a deck. This duty would be the second and last command of my air force career.

As compartment commander I was given an assistant who turned out to be far more an advisor than an assistant. He was a master sergeant whose name was Gallagher. Until we reached Manila, the two of us were charged with the welfare of those soldiers and marines. And with all due respect for my rank, Sergeant Gallagher took me on as his student in an informal course on practical military administration, a course that for ages past has been taught by sergeants to second lieutenants.

The Philippine part of the adventure began for me on the night we docked, when I took a room in the Manila Hotel, a grand old pile known in that part of the world as "The Pearl of the Orient" while my compadres passed up the romance of the Manila for the Bay Shore on Dewey Boulevard. The romance of the Manila Hotel included a mosquito net under which I slept and a diagonal line of submachine gun bullet holes on the wall just inside the door that were left over from our 1945 reoccupation of the Philippines. "The Pearl of the Orient" had seen better days.

The next part of the adventure was of quite a different nature, and romantic only in the sense that it illuminates the fortunes and misfortunes of war. The day after our arrival in Manila Bay we were taken by bus to Clark Field, where we were assigned quarters and duty offices, and where, to our consternation, we were told that Colonel Arnold together with a dozen or so of his officers and airmen had been shot down over enemy territory and were now in the hands of the Red Chinese. The implications of this incident, the capture of the commander of the highly covert 581st, were appalling. The "shoot-down," as it was called, had occurred during a night mission on January 12, 1953, and 581st headquarters at Clark was notified through secret channels on the morning of the 13th. The colonel's plane—call name *Stardust 40*—was

Crew of the *Stardust 40* at Mountain Home Air Force Base, 1952 (courtesy John W. Thompson, USAF)

one of our own Mountain Home B-29s that had been flown across the Pacific the previous July.

Later we would learn that Colonel Arnold and the rest of the crew were subjected to months of torture by the Chinese, and that they were tried and convicted of waging "germ warfare." Two years after the end of the war, following secret meetings of U.S. and Red Chinese diplomats in Geneva, the prisoners were finally released. Beyond these facts, parts of the whole episode are opaque even now. Haas (1997) questions how the shoot-down actually occurred. He writes that perhaps the Red Chinese knew ahead of time that Arnold was aboard *Stardust 40* and says, "If true, this knowledge would represent the highest possible security breach." Further, he remarks, "The bizarre circumstances of the shoot-down and the continued torture of the surviving *Stardust 40* crew members, even *after* [italics his] the war concluded raised questions that remain unanswered to this day." As I will explain later in this chapter, the circumstances of the catastrophic incident became murkier and more personal in the weeks following our arrival in the Philippines. Even so, with Colonel Lawrence C. Gilbert, who had been deputy wing commander under Colonel Arnold, as its new commander, the endeavors of the 581st at Clark Field seemed to flow on with hardly a ripple.

Compared with Mountain Home, Clark Air Force Base (known universally in military and naval circles as "Clark Field") was a five-star resort. The old parade ground, left over from those faraway horse-soldier days when Clark Field was a U.S. Army post, was lined with scarlet-blossomed, sweet-smelling frangipani trees. Everywhere there were bananas, palms, and other jungly things. A giant iguana lived in a patch of dense forest on our eighteen-hole golf course, where once in a while we would find him foraging on a fairway. Wild jungle fowl lived among the bananas on Lily Hill, a bump in the center of the base that contained our radar apparatus. We lived in a BOQ occupied by first and second lieutenants in which we were looked after by Filipino houseboys to whom we paid a few dollars a week for doing our "small items" such as making our beds, shining our shoes, and laundering our socks and underwear. To avoid the worst of the tropical heat we reported for duty at 0700 hours each morning and knocked off in the middle of the afternoon for the pool at the officers' club.

In 1953 Clark Field, which as I write this in 2008 lies abandoned under volcanic ash from the 1991 eruption of neighboring Mount Pinatubo, had a fenced and guarded perimeter of several miles. In addition to patches of jungle and savannah, buildings of various styles that together spanned more than half a century of military occupation still stood. After having won the Spanish American War of 1898, the United States paid Spain twenty million dollars for the Philippine Islands. Here, at what was now Clark Field, Fort Stotsenberg was established in 1903. In 1919 a landing strip called Clark Field was built on a small fraction of Fort Stotsenberg's expansive grounds. In 1949, four years after the end of the Second World War, the entire fort was named Clark Air Base, and soon afterward, with the formal creation of the U.S. Air Force, the name became Clark Air Force Base.

In the 1950s this evolution was reflected in an assortment of architectural designs, among the most curious of which were buildings left behind by the Japanese. On December 7, 1941, Clark Field was home to an array of U.S. Army aircraft consisting of two groups and five squadrons of bombers and fighters, the latter known as pursuit planes. All of them, within a few hours of the bombing of Pearl Harbor, were destroyed on the ground or in the air by nearly simultaneous Japanese attacks. In 1953, reminders of the subsequent Japanese occupation of Clark Field included a Zero, the famous Japanese fighter plane, perched on a pylon beside Clark's operations tower. Quite a few of the curious single-story Japanese buildings of Philippine mahogany and bamboo-slat con-struction also remained. The structures were rather elegant, though they were probably the product of forced labor, and both our 581st duty offices and the base officers' club were housed in these souvenirs of the enemy. In fact, our officers' club had been built by the Japanese for that same purpose.

Adding further to Clark's exotic appeal were two bands of Negritos, the diminutive blacks who quite possibly have occupied the Philippines for ten thousand years or more. Living in pole and grass huts in two little camps on

Author and Negrito hunter in Luzon rain forest, 1953 (photo by Paquing Tolentino)

the edge of the jungle near opposite ends of the base, they grew a tropical root vegetable called taro in small openings in the deep forest, which they cleared by slashing and burning. They also hunted deer and wild pigs with bows and arrows and wore very little in the way of clothing.

The jungle was a textbook tropical rain forest whose towering canopy left its floor in such perpetual shadow that little besides lichens and mosses grew beneath the trees. Here my shotgun, which I had shipped over the ocean in my footlocker, was a delight to the Negritos. While they carried their bows and arrows, they much preferred to call down within range of the gun bleeding-heart pigeons, a bird so named because of a blood-red patch of feathers on its breast.

The deer and pigs lived in big upland fields of cogon, a dense, sharp-edged native grass growing ten feet tall, which bordered the jungle and was practically impenetrable to humankind. Following the monsoon rains, when the cogon dried out these same hunters set it afire, driving out the animals and killing them with arrows. I was not invited on these hunts, but on the clear, dark nights of the dry season we could see the wandering fire lines from the old parade ground that bordered the club.

I wangled time with the Negritos largely because of my BA in anthropology. The brass at Clark took a certain satisfaction from having a so-called anthropologist around. They even gave me a "Negrito Project" or two. In the days scattered over several months that I spent with them, I composed a paper, published years afterward, that described their magical uses of stone adz blades. These blades had been made by farmers of the Southeast Asian Neolithic, some five thousand years ago. The Negritos would occasionally find them lying on the floor of the jungle and, knowing nothing about the Southeast Asian Neolithic, they believed they had fallen from the sky in tropical lightning storms. In collecting field data for this project I depended on the help of a remarkable man named Paquing Tolentino. Middle-aged, he was the son of a Negrito mother and an American black soldier father who had been stationed at Fort Stotsenberg in the early nineteen hundreds. He spoke Tagalog and English, as well as his mother's language, and he became my indispensable adviser and interpreter.

As remarkable as Paquing Tolentino, but for another reason, was the full-blooded Negrito man we saw from time to time in the Clark Officers' Club. In 1953 (and probably still, unless they have since become assimilated in the larger Philippine gene pool) regional Negrito men were on average less than four and a half feet tall. Negrito women were shorter by five inches. If anything this small man was shorter than average, but dressed in cut-down and taken-in air force summer shorts and blouse. He wore on his shoulders the silver leaves of a lieutenant colonel and he was addressed as "Colonel" by one and all of us.

As it came to us from American officers (he spoke no English, and I never knew his name), his was an interesting story. During the Second World War the Negritos were treated miserably by the Japanese, a policy and practice that resulted in furtive and bloody retaliation. This particular black man had got even by hiding late one night behind a palm, which still stood in front of what had become our officers' club, and with his bolo (machete) lopping off the heads of two of the more senior club members. Among the Pinatubo Negritos, as those of this region were called, his accomplishment was one of a number of outstanding examples of Negrito guerilla warfare. At the end of the war General Douglas MacArthur, supreme commander of Allied forces in the Southwest Pacific, recognized their valor in several ways, including inviting one band to set up headquarters under the protection of Clark's miles-long perimeter fence, and awarding this hero the honorary rank of lieutenant colonel.

In addition to getting semiofficial sanction for the magical adz project, I finagled some birding. Besides the bleeding-heart pigeons and the mallards I bagged on the nearby Bamban River, I "took" other species with my binoculars. As an interesting adjunct to these pursuits at Clark there was the birding on Dewey Boulevard in Manila, where I bought live sandpipers from vendors who netted them at night by the light of bonfires on the shores of Manila Bay. Peddled at curbside, the birds were sold mainly to servants of wealthy Chinese who for generations had lived in Manila and who were fond of eating sandpipers. I turned mine into study skins that later found their way to Chicago's Field Museum of Natural History.

As appealing as were these exotic pastimes, they were beside the point of what the 581st was doing at Clark. From our first day we were made aware of how much duty here differed from that at Mountain Home, especially as concerned white hats and black hats. Unlike the invisible line of demarcation that at Mountain Home had physically and operationally separated us, at Clark our respective duty offices were intermingled in what amounted to a compound without a wall around it. Here, the same narrow asphalt sidewalks led to "open" buildings, in which we composers of leaflets and radio messages worked, and other buildings whose locked doors were guarded by armed airmen. This proximity of offices resulted in a casual camaraderie among "blacks" and "whites," and additionally came to mean an official overlapping of our purposes.

One of our Clark Field white-hat projects called for the construction (with the guidance of U.S. Army experts sent down from Japan) of an actual leaflet machine with which we could turn out real leaflets. Try as we might (I use *we* in the editorial sense; I had nothing to do with this particular project), we could only get the machine to produce one leaflet at a time instead of the multiple hundreds and thousands for which it was designed. When we were visited by senior intelligence officers from other bases, our brass would show off the machine, which, after its one leaflet, would be shut down suddenly because "Gentlemen, they are waiting for us at Thirteenth Headquarters," or something similar.

However, very little of our on-base training related to composing leaflet or radio messages. Most of what we learned reflected the overlap of white-hat and black-hat operations. For me, classwork amounted mainly to a lengthy informal course in what might be called "Escape and Evasion," in which I was the only student, taught by a lieutenant colonel who was both an expert on jungles and a black hat.

Past middle age, Lieutenant Colonel Hedrick was a "retread" called back to active duty after having spent much of the last war rescuing aircrews who had gone down in the jungles of India and Burma while flying the "Hump" (the American-British air supply route across the Himalayas). Until I came along, his staff was composed of three other officers, a major, a captain, and a first lieutenant, all black hats whose duties were not revealed to me. My lessons from Colonel Hedrick were derived from his experiences in the jungles, experiences that related to the mission of the 581st, in that they had to do with how he had got along with remote native people and how he had persuaded them to help him in his searches for downed U.S. flyers even while they were also being sought out by agents of the Japanese.

As I entered the door each morning he would say, "Campbell!" and after the saluting he would have me pull up a chair to his desk where with pad and pen I listened and took notes. Soon I became as attentive and loyal a second lieutenant as that gray-haired spellbinder had ever had under his wing, but one morning he told us that he had orders to report to "Washington" and that was the last we ever saw of him. It was marvelous getting acquainted with these sorts of genuine spooks who often seemed to be going off to "Washington," even though we never got to know them very well.

Among the 581st people who occupied one of the buildings to which we were not permitted entry was a nameless middle-aged master sergeant. Each morning on our arriving from opposite directions on our respective ways to work, we would meet on one of the walks leading through our duty compound, where with correct military courtesy he would salute me with "Good morning, Lieutenant"; returning his salute, I would say, "Good morning, Sergeant." One morning as we approached on the path, it occurred to me that there was something different about the sergeant. The something different was that instead of stripes and chevrons on his arm he was wearing eagles on his shoulders, the silver eagles of a full "bird" colonel. I managed a flabbergasted salute, which he returned with his usual "Good morning, Lieutenant." Courteous as ever, he explained that his permanent rank was master sergeant, but that sometimes temporarily he was a colonel and in that rank he was on his way to "Washington."[4]

In the case of First Lieutenant Drexel "Barney" Cochran, we were to learn that his "Washington" was somewhere north of Seoul (I knew Barney from our mutual interest in archaeology). We knew nothing at all about the frequent off-base whereabouts of other black hats, among whom was an affable lieutenant colonel known in the wing as "Steady Eddy Sustrick, the Friendly Guerilla Chieftain."

In addition to these ephemeral acquaintances with real spooks, we white hats were to have other adventures at Clark that differed notably from anything we had experienced at Mountain Home. These were off-base assignments of two quite different types and purposes: social or political excursions, whose purpose was that of impressing the Filipinos with the good will of the U.S. Air Force, and secretive missions, relating to the war that in our orders were referred to as concerning "intelligence matters."[5]

Ordinarily we were given the social assignments verbally by one or another 581st or Thirteenth Air Force officer. The first for me was a request that I attend, in full dress uniform—white shirt, black bow tie, and all—a lavish Manila wedding reception at which I was the only American guest. On another similar mission and again in full dress, I was introduced to His Excellency Elpidio Quirino, president of the Philippines, in his palace of Malacañang, whose marble floors were strewn quite amazingly with dozens of tiger skins brought down for that purpose from the jungles of mainland East Asia.

That occasion honored a glittering array of scholars who were in Manila for the Eighth Pacific Science Conference. Because no senior officer was interested, I represented the 581st and the Thirteenth Air Force. Attending stars, among others, included Julian Huxley, the English biologist; Gustav Von Koenigswald of *Pithecanthropus* "Java man" fame; and George Peter Murdock, the internationally known ethnographer and chairman of anthropology at Yale. Following the president's reception I had the great good luck to become acquainted further with Professor Murdock when we were seated together at dinner, and that chance meeting was to have a profound effect on my future career. Two years later, when I was home and out of uniform, he invited me to apply for admittance to Yale's PhD program in anthropology.

Our missions relative to "intelligence matters" covered an array of brief, data-collecting assignments for which we were given both verbal instructions and standard, if opaque, TDY orders. Some of these adventures were far-flung, one of them taking a fellow lieutenant clear to Taiwan and back. Others were close to home and less formally initiated. On one occasion, I was told that on my next trip to Manila I was to ask a new acquaintance of mine—an Englishman and an "Old China Hand"—what he might know of rail yards in the Red Chinese province of Kiangsu directly across the Yellow Sea from Korea. Another adventure involved my being assigned as anthropologist observer to an exceedingly low-level reconnaissance in a 581st SA-16 Albatross of a beach and river mouth on the little-known northeast tip of Luzon.

This odd mission related to a sea-air search for the murderers of three U.S. Navy men. Because we were warned to keep our mouths shut, we knew little of one another's assignments. As far as I know, all these sorts of duties were low level and ancillary to, but not directly a part of, the far more arcane operations of the 581st, which were planned and hatched in our cluster of old Japanese buildings but were kept hidden from us.

The missions of our black hats, or "special operations agents" as they would be called today, rotating through Clark would remain a mystery to us as well as to most of the rest of the world until after the Korean armistice and in some cases decades after the close of the war. To this day details of certain operations are obscured either by the passage of time or by deliberate censorship.

SA-16 Albatross in low flight off beach on northern Luzon, 1953 (photo by author)

However, available published sources and personal correspondence with air force veterans illuminate some of the black-hat activities of ARCS and other special operations personnel assigned to covert missions in Korea.[6]

The help of Korean partisans was essential to any psywar mission conducted behind enemy lines. Whether assignments from Clark allotted members of the 581st to detachments responsible for inserting agents in the heart of enemy territory, appropriating Russian-made arms for technical intelligence, sabotaging airfields, or rescuing downed pilots and whether they became known as bandit chiefs (apropos of Steady Eddy Sustrick), spymasters, or simply spooks, their achievements would have been impossible without the cooperation and determination of Korean agents.

The ladies of Madam Rhee's theater arts circle stepped from the stylish clothes and comfortable surroundings of Korean prewar high society that surrounded the newly elected president of South Korea, Syngman Rhee, and his Austrian-born wife, into parachute harnesses and the jump-seats of bombers bound deep into North Korea. Once "inserted," in the dark of night these women, bundled now in padded cotton suits "borrowed" beforehand from captured Chinese and North Korean troops, would make their way to assigned enemy military command posts to charm information out of officers of sufficient rank and power to lead attacks on UN forces. Then, armed only with their wits and their precious information (they carried neither weapons nor radios), these women had to disappear discreetly into the chaos of shifting battle-lines to be captured and interned as UN POWs. If all went well, their prearranged code words would bring a quick pick-up by an intelligence case officer. In one instance, a movie actress would have won rave reviews from the soldiers of the Second Division of the U.S. Army if they had known the marines sent to reinforce them had been ordered to their position based on information she had gleaned while sleeping with a Chinese lieutenant colonel. The colonel had sought to impress her by revealing an eighty-mile side step in his attack that would have allowed Chinese forces to pour through the paper-thin U.S. line.

As we now know, some of our casual acquaintances at Clark had been allotted in small numbers to detachments of the Fifth Air Force 6004th Air Intelligence Service Squadron (AISS) for "operational training." In many instances, their missions were coordinated and commanded by Major Donald Nichols, often at the request of General Earle E. Partridge, commander of the Fifth Air Force. Nichols's network of partisan agents had been in place before the invasion by North Korea (see introduction). The trust and value the Fifth Air Force in Korea and the Far East Air Force in Japan placed in Nichols, his partisans, and his trade-craft as a spymaster could be measured more easily by the men and material they put at his command than by any insignia he wore. This collaboration between General Partridge and Nichols was given air force designation as the 6004th Air Intelligence Service Squadron. The 6004th, which would eventually hold three detachments, became one of the primary assignments of officers allotted from the 581st Resupply, Communications, and Holding and Briefing squadrons.

By the time my group of 581st stragglers got settled at Clark, every branch of the American military plus the CIA were running clandestine operations in Korea. As per its design, our wing served as a depot and one-stop shop allotting pilots and aircraft, as well as propagandists, to UN Command Forces, the Far Eastern Air Force, the Fifth Air Force, and the catchall of combined command, CCRAK, which handled clandestine, covert, and reconnaissance activities in Korea. So many special operations and covert missions were launched by aircraft parked at Seoul City Air Base, also designated as K-16—its UN Command number—that the field became known as "Spook City" to U.S. ground personnel and pilots whether they were involved in psychological warfare or regular military assignments.

Among the aircraft with the odd paint (black or dark grey) that flew night missions from K-16 were four H-119A helicopters. They belonged to the 581st

ARCS Helicopter Squadron (581st ARSq [H]), but since the 581st was classified and known only by Fifth Air Force Intelligence to have the squadron in Korea, the Third Air Rescue Group in Japan or the 2157th Air Rescue Squadron based at K-16 fostered the orphans. Between the normal military bedlam of conducting war and the designed confusion of launching covert special operations, the 581st *seemed* to have misplaced four helicopters, six pilots, one NCO, and twelve enlisted men.

Although the mysterious helicopter squadron (carefully parked between air rescue units at K-16 and the grim, black-painted transports and short-range bombers of B-Flight in "Spook City") was busy with rescue operations during the day and agent insertion at night, their activities and location went unreported among those at Clark concerned with pay and promotions. Some crew members were listed as AWOL and others were locked into ratings and served past discharge dates. The commander of the 2157th Air Rescue, while acknowledging the teams' skill at snagging pilots from the frozen lakes and rugged coastlines of North Korea and the perilous waters of the Yellow Sea, was insistent that the rescue markings be removed from their helicopters. The daylight rescue of the ace fighter pilot Joe McConnell by one of the unmarked helicopters had to be "staged" on a lake in Japan before a photo could be released to *Pacific Stars and Stripes*. It was even more difficult for the Fifth Air Force to explain why a gray helicopter made "the deepest helicopter penetration of the war into North Korea just to empty the trash." Yet they must have come up with something because the "rinky-dink" trash-hauling rescue squadron continued with its significant contribution to psychological warfare in deep cover throughout the war.

The 581st Helicopter Squadron's answer to questions about their mysterious journeys was that they were hauling "ash and trash, and dogs and cats" (Sullivan 1995).[7] That seemed to take care of idle curiosity as well as the pointed scrutiny of regular military officialdom. However, the depth of cover adapted by both the military and the CIA was often at cross-purposes, and the strategy of collocating black-hat and white-hat aircraft and agents was occasionally counterproductive or worse. Regular military actions in Korea as well as our white-hat air force missions became unknowingly entwined in covert operations, sometimes to the detriment of both and the advantage of the enemy.

As the UN Command Forces were ordered to stand fast on or near the 38th parallel, Chinese and North Korean leaders tightened security north of the line. Both white-hat and black-hat flights into the North came under increasingly deadly attacks not only by Russian-made MIG-15 fighters, which shot down five B-29s in the last four months of 1952, but by the sabotage of double agents. Events surrounding the shoot-down of *Stardust 40* illustrate not only the depth to which the Chinese and most likely the Russians had penetrated 581st covert operations, but the levels of cover used by both sides.

The *Stardust 40* was a B-29 stripped of armament and refitted for leaflet missions at Mountain Home Air Force Base, then flown to Clark in the Philippines. From Clark the *Stardust 40* was rotated to a base in Yokota, Japan, where it was operated and maintained by the Ninety-first Strategic Reconnaissance Squadron. Complete with its leaflet-dropping assembly and black paint, the *Stardust 40* pursued its psywar missions along the North Korean/Manchurian border using the cover of the reconnaissance squadron in much the same manner as the helicopter squadron based at K-16. It was the commander of the Ninety-first Strategic Reconnaissance Squadron that informed Clark of the shoot-down and the loss of the crew and the commander of the 581st. While we white hats just arriving at Clark had concerns about the loss of our wing commander on an "operational training" and leaflet mission, CIA contacts within our wing Resupply Squadron had reason to believe operations far beyond leafleting were at risk.

In a meeting with the UN Secretary General in January 1955, the senior Chinese negotiator, Chou En-lai, came as close to explaining the continued imprisonment of the crew as he was allowed to admit. The Air Resupply and Communications Service was, he explained, merely an extension of the CIA. In a revelation that would have interested those of us white hats at Clark who had never set foot at Fort Benning, Chou linked CIA and *all* 581st training to the special forces school in Georgia. The psychological warfare teams, he added, were simply used as a cover.

In the months following the deployment of our wing to the Philippines in the summer of 1952, small cadres of junior 581st officers had been sent up to Korea in rotation for "on-the-job training" in psychological warfare with the U.S. Army. These particular TDY tours typically involved five weeks or more, counting time en route. They were also not without certain hazards to the participants, a fair number of whom had been bombed or shot at by the North Koreans or Red Chinese. Lieutenant Charlie Grill had come back to Clark with a Bronze Star. Now for the first time since the capture of Colonel Arnold and crew, it was rumored that another cadre was being ordered out, but his loss had attached an additional hazard to this kind of duty in Korea. As junior officers our knowledge of the shoot-down was naturally even more scanty and inaccurate than that of the higher ups. The 581st brass were understandably keeping quiet about whatever further details they may have known, but the story going around Clark was that *Stardust 40* had actually been shot down on the Red Chinese side of the Yalu River, not the North Korean side as the United

States claimed, and that Colonel Arnold and his crew were to be tried and shot as war criminals. Further, and of particular interest to prospective members of any future cadres, the story had it that from now on all captured 581st officers and airmen would get the same treatment.

This dire possibility notwithstanding, on May 19 seven of us were handed copies of a "Special Orders." Suitably vague, and signed by the adjutant and assistant adjutant of the 581st "By Order of Colonel Gilbert," and in typical air force shorthand, they began with "Fol named off, Hq 581st Air Resupply & Com Wg, this sta, APO 74, WP Hq 5th AF (Adv), APO 970 o/a 23 may 53 on important TDY for aprx 28 days for purpose of tng. Upon compl of TDY off w/ rtrn to proper sta." Further, the orders noted that we were cleared for access to classified materials "up to and incl SECRET," and among other administrative details they directed us in such matters as drawing field clothing and equipment and getting inoculated for mainland East Asia diseases. That was all. These Special Orders neither told us the location of Fifth Air Force Adv. [Advance] nor how we were going to get there.

Chapter Four

Korea

On the appointed day we left Clark in a C-124, one of the large military transport planes of those years, which was powered by four radial gasoline engines. Because of its bulbous proportions, the C-124 was often called the Pregnant Guppy. Flying northward over the Philippine Sea, we stopped briefly on Okinawa for refueling and late in the afternoon landed at the U.S. Tachikawa Air Base near Tokyo. Two days afterward we were driven across Tachikawa's runways to a waiting C-47, the venerable twin-engine work-horse known as the Gooney Bird, which had been in service since the 1930s. Unlike our flight over the sea in the C-124, whose numerous travelers included two dozen military chaplains on their way to a conference in Japan, we seven were the C-47's only passengers, a circumstance that we supposed reflected on our membership in the elusive 581st. Piloted by two air force lieutenants, we flew westward across the Japanese home islands of Honshu, Shikoku, and Kyushu, then north across the Korea Strait to the southern tip of Korea and on northward up the Korean Peninsula. Supposedly we were still unaware of our destination, but by then we had gleaned that it was most probably K-16, the "Spook Base" noted in chapter 3. In perfectly clear, calm weather, flying well under ten thousand feet above sea level, it was a lovely scenic flight until in the dusk of early evening, on our low approach to K-16, the seven of us got our first introduction to a shooting war when the sky around us was filled suddenly with the bursts of antiaircraft shells.

Some of the peoples' names in this chapter have been changed.

Pontoon bridge across the Han River, June 1953 (photo by author)

All of South Korea had been Allied domain since March 1951, and this terrifying barrage from one of our own antiaircraft batteries had resulted from a brief breakdown in the local IFF (Identify Friend or Foe) radio code apparatus, whose failure prompted the battery to try to shoot us down. We landed unscathed. The only casualty in this example of "friendly fire" was a civilian reporter for *Life* or *Look* who, while dashing out of a nearby war correspondents' tent to see what was going on, was wounded in the leg by a piece of falling flak.

Once on the ground we were met by an air force captain who said he was expecting us. After examining our orders, he handed us over to the corporal driver of a weapons carrier, our transportation to the headquarters of Fifth Air Force Advance, which lay some miles away on the other side of Seoul. Fifth Air Force Advance was quartered in parts of the old Japanese University of Chosen.[1] Our billet for the duration of our Korean tour was to be in a hospital building that had belonged to the university's medical school.

We reached our destination by a meandering route, most of which was known to our driver, but it was late at night when we got there, and not knowing much about the layout of the Fifth's headquarters he let us out in front of a little building that had housed the school's surgical amphitheater. A marble-topped table stood in the center of the small circular room and around it, in ascending circles, were the tiered benches once occupied by medical students. Rolling out our issue blankets, we spent our first night here, after arguing over who was to get the operating table instead of the curved bleachers.

The next morning we found our way to the old building, whose rooms had once held hospital patients but which was now a makeshift BOQ and the office and quarters of a Major Scott, who served as 581st (Thirteenth Air Force) liaison to both Fifth Air Force and Eighth Army. The amiable major, who was to treat us like younger brothers, assigned us rooms and handed each of us a mimeographed copy of an order signed by Col. Hall, "Chief [Eighth Army], Psywar." Brief and otherwise uninformative, it assigned us individually to components of either the Fifth Air Force or Eighth Army Psywar effort, i.e., Intelligence, Operations, Leaflets, and Loudspeakers. I drew Operations (army), which was to give me a close look at a variety of Eighth Army combat enterprises, including some that had nothing to do with psywar. These were the only written orders we would get during our several weeks in Korea. The others were delivered verbally by either Major Scott or one or another army or air force officer.

Eighth Army and Fifth Air Force headquarters, commanded respectively by Lieutenant General Maxwell D. Taylor and Lieutenant General Samuel E. Anderson,[2] consisted of clusters of both U.S. "temporaries" and old Korean and Japanese buildings that were almost directly across a gravel road from one another. Our billet at Fifth Air Force was "home" in the sense of being where we ate and slept between adventures with the army or air force. From here, those of us who had drawn army duty were ordered out on separate assignments. Each of us was the only air force member of whatever army outfit was our host, and because we wore army field dress, only our escorts were aware of our masquerade.

Some assignments were close to home. For me, the first of these required that on three successive mornings I report to a daily briefing at Eighth Army, across the road, in which an army colonel—not of Psywar—was appraised of how the battle had gone during the past twenty-four hours. Each day a few minutes before 0730 hours, a dozen field-grade army officers and I were admitted to a one-room shack guarded by a sergeant who matched our names with those on his clipboard, examined our dog tags, and ushered us into the room. Except for folding chairs and four or five large maps covered over with sheets of brown paper on its back wall, the room was bare. In front of the hidden maps, which we faced from our chairs, stood a short, impeccable army captain. When at precisely 0730 hours the colonel walked in, the captain would boom "Attention!" We would snap to our feet, the colonel would say, "Thank you, Captain; as you were, Gentlemen," and when he had taken his front row seat we would sit down again.

Then, one at a time, the captain would uncover and explain his battle situation maps. He addressed his remarks to "Sir," meaning the colonel, and always his presentation was sheer, if understated, drama. Speaking without

Main Supply Route northeast of Uijongbu, June 1953 (photo by author)

flourish or embellishment, he would show and tell us the details of the previous day's fighting. Because the war was winding down and both sides were jockeying for advantage, the fighting was sometimes bloody. When the captain was finished, the colonel asked a question or two. Then he would say, "Thank you, Captain," the captain would bring us to attention, the two of them would exchange salutes, and the colonel would stride out the door. They were brilliant performances, but after the third morning, Major Scott told me that the next day I was to report across the street to Eighth Army G3 (Psywar).

At G3, I was told to come back after lunch in field gear: boots, helmet, pistol, and with enough extra shirts, socks, and underwear "for a few days up north." That afternoon I was sent off by jeep to an unannounced destination that turned out to be headquarters of Eighth Army's First Corps. First Corps had as its numerical designation the Roman numeral *I*, for which it was called "Eye" Corps. Its 45,000 men (in divisions, regiments, battalions, and companies) were scattered among the Korean hills along the MLR, the Main Line of Resistance, known most commonly as "the Line." Its headquarters, an orderly sprawl of olive-drab tents, occupied a small valley near the town of Uijonbu. To get there we traveled northward on the Main Supply Route (MSR). The MSR was a broad improved road, the artery of military transport from Seoul and its environs to the welter of lesser roads and tracks branching off to various sectors of the line of battle.

It was surfaced with pale gravel and clay, pale enough that on moonlit nights, as I will describe further, it allowed for driving without headlights. My driver, a corporal, said that Eye Corps was blacked out from dark till dawn and that, if we were to get there in daylight, we would have to hurry. Upon our arrival, a lieutenant directed us to our respective billets and in half an hour perimeter sentries were out and the camp was dark as a tomb. Eye Corps Headquarters was a few miles south of the MLR. Many of its scattered units as well as those of other UN fighting forces strung out across the width of Korea were even closer to the Line. For all of them blackouts were the rule.

Possible trouble in the middle of the night included attacks by both conventional enemy forces and infiltrators who sneaked down from the north for purposes of bushwhacking or of gathering intelligence. The latter related especially to the positions and strengths of UN army units tucked away among the hills on our side of the Line. By May 1953, enemy spotting-planes had all but disappeared from where the fighting was going on and were unheard of south of the MLR. Accordingly, the North Koreans and Red Chinese depended on their spies and on UN prisoners for these sorts of essential data. Most threatening to the peace of mind of our forward detachments were the bushwhackers, military or civilian, who in the dark stalked the unwary soldier. Hence the universal blackouts that, outside the double doors of the heavy canvas tents, applied to all lights down to and including lighted cigarettes.

In the morning I reported to a tent occupied by a captain and a staff sergeant. The captain was sitting at a small table, the sergeant standing beside it. In those weeks in Korea, neither I nor my air force fellow travelers were told ahead of time what or where our next assignments would be and as I have mentioned we always got our orders verbally. The captain said that in the immediate future my duties were to get acquainted with G3 operations on the Line and that Sergeant Oletta (a war-wise soldier who spoke classic Brooklynese) would be my escort.

Beginning with that first day's drive from Eighth Army to Eye Corps, nearly all of the country north of Seoul through which I would travel—always by jeep—was a landscape of dry hills cut by small valleys and narrow canyons. The once heavily forested hills had been logged for countless generations, most recently in small part by UN and Communist armies for the raw materials of trenchworks, bunkers, and bridges. The dry, sparse, open woods reminded me of much of New Mexico. Sergeant Oletta and I started off on the MSR and then drove onto a smaller dirt road, which led to an even smaller one that wound down among the hills to the Imjin River, spanned by a narrow bridge built of wood and steel by our Corps of Engineers. Here the Imjin was a little river of clear deep pools. Across the bridge at the end of the road was a hut,

On the MLR, June 1953. From left to right: author, Corporal Brian, Sergeant Oletta, ROK soldier Kim (photographer unidentified)

dug into the base of a steep ridge and made of logs and empty howitzer-shell boxes filled with sand from the river.

We had come to the Main Line of Resistance, and while we were in territory held then by the UN, back down the road we had crossed the 38th parallel of north latitude into country that since the war has belonged to North Korea. The several hundred feet from the hut to the top of the ridge were ours. Beyond that was the Chorwon Valley, and on its other side was the North Korean Peoples Army (NKPA). The hut's four inhabitants, who had been alerted to our impending visit by field radio, were two American corporals and a South Korean soldier who went by the name of Kim.

Our final destination was a frontline "broadcasting studio" sited on the northern enemy-facing slope of the ridge above us. As tranquil as this glade by the river seemed to be, it was in fact in the line of fire. The four men were wearing "flak vests," olive-drab sleeveless jackets lined with overlapping plates of Doron designed to stop fragments of shrapnel and assorted small-caliber bullets. That morning before our arrival an enemy artillery shell had exploded on the river's bank. Kim gave me a piece of its shrapnel that had fallen in front of the dugout, which I use still as a war souvenir paperweight. And after donning identical vests from a box of extras, the sergeant and I climbed a steep trail up the ridge.

At its top, Oletta said that we were now in sight of the NKPA and that we would lie low in a convenient shell hole while he got a better idea of what was going on across the way on the enemy side. The view from the hole was impressive. Getting on toward mid-afternoon of a perfectly calm day, we looked across the valley through wisps of smoke left by white phosphorous shells fired from U.S. jet fighters a few minutes earlier. As the crow flies, the distance from our perch to the North Korean ridge was a little less than a mile, out of range of effective rifle fire. With our binoculars (the sergeant's army issue and mine a small pair of hunting glasses I had brought with me from the States), we saw plainly the opposing barren hogback, so much like our own, including that it showed no sign of soldiers.

East and west as far as we could see, the valley had been scoured by artillery and mortar fire in pitched battles that now had devolved to an occasional probe or skirmish by thin infantry units holding their respective opposite ridges and keeping their heads down. However, this holding of the Line involved more than lying low in convenient shell holes. In the lull that had followed the heavy fighting—a lull that in this sector would prevail until the cease-fire—troops of both sides had dug trenches and built semisubterranean bunkers. Primitive as they were, they provided relative comfort and protection in the face-to-face standoff.

Our objective, the broadcasting studio, was one of our own bunkers. Dug in the dark of the moon, it lay one hundred yards downslope in front of us. To reach it we had to run down over open ground for half that distance to the entrance of a deep trench leading on to the bunker. Roofed with logs covered with two feet of dirt and walled and floored with assorted secondhand plywood boards, the studio was perhaps twelve feet square and from floor to ceiling seven feet high. Facing the NKPA, a narrow horizontal slit at eye level was covered with chicken wire camouflaged with strips of earth-colored cloth.

At that time of day the bunker's only occupant was an army sergeant. An acquaintance of Sergeant Oletta's, he had been waiting for us. He began by saying that he hoped the bunker had gone unnoticed by the NKPA. Either that, he said, or because his broadcasts had not made any converts so far, the North Koreans had decided against trying to wipe it out. The room was furnished with a few homemade chairs and a homemade table on top of which stood a state-of-the-art microphone powered by heavy batteries stored in wood boxes on the floor. The sergeant explained that the mike was connected to a wire laid downslope over the churned ground for several hundred feet, nearly to the bottom of the valley, where it was connected to a camouflaged loudspeaker. He added that "getting the son of a bitch down there, even in the dark, was a little hairy." The routine, he told me, was that each night Kim would come to sit in front of the mike. Reading from script, or sometimes going it on his own, he would try to persuade the NKPA soldiers to come over to our side. Kim's pitch, which varied from night to night primarily in that it included daily news, conformed generally to our leaflet messages described in chapter 5. To wit: the onerous presence of the Red Chinese Army in North Korea, the comfort and safety afforded NKPA deserters by UN forces, the futility of prolonging the war, etc. But he had yet to get any takers.

After an hour of briefing by the generously knowledgeable sergeant, Sergeant Oletta and I dashed back over the top of the ridge, where as a grand finale to my first day in "combat," I was given the further novel experience of listening in on an artillery duel. It began with three or four loud booms from heavy guns hidden nearby on our side of the Line. "One five five howitzers,"[3] said Oletta. As he was getting the words out, odd ripping sounds came to us from close overhead: sounds of the guns' projectiles on their way over and across the valley to enemy targets lying well behind the MLR. In a few moments we heard answering booms, muted and dull in the distance, from Soviet-built howitzers, Oletta said. Then, moments later, the sounds of their shells exploding down in the sparse woods behind us.

After two such exchanges, the artillerymen called it a draw and quit for the afternoon. We never learned the damage, if any, our barrage had done to the enemy battery or whatever else our target may have been, and we were told later that their incoming shells had ruined only a grove of Korean pines. At dusk we retrieved our jeep and drove home to Eye Corps, the last few miles in blackout down the pale MSR.

There were further adventures with Oletta, including one in which he took me up to watch a 155 battery roar away at the NKPA with its ninety-five-pound shells, and another when he nearly shot a drunken U.S. marine who lunged at us one night on the MSR and who, we naturally thought, was a bushwhacker. The most delightful of such incidents, however, was my intro-duction to a British battalion by the savvy sergeant, whose knowledge of war included the tidbit that frontline British officers' and sergeants' messes served *liquor*, an amenity that in forward combat zones was denied, at least officially, to American soldiers and sailors. I learned of this practice of our closest ally when two days after our visit to the broadcasting bunker, we were back on a neighboring part of the Line. Toward the end of the afternoon, Oletta said he happened to know of a Brit infantry battalion bivouacked among the hills behind and west of us and that on our way to Eye Corps that evening we might like to drop by during the dinner hour.

To reach the British battalion, which had recently been pulled off the Line, we took a dirt road. A narrow track that followed the crests of the ridges

on our side of the Chorwon Valley, it was occasionally marked with white signs, each of which contained a drawing in black.

The sergeant explained that the man peering over the fence was "Moe" (the enemy), that each sign meant we were in a spot where Moe could see us from where he sat across the valley, and that we should step on the gas for a few yards until we would be out of sight again on our side of the ridge.

At dusk on this same road, a dim figure jumped from beneath some scraggly trees in front of us, pointing a carbine and yelling, "Halt!" We halted and Oletta turned off the ignition. "Give the password!" shouted the shadowy figure in what to my ear was the same language as the sergeant's Brooklynese. There was a nervous silence, broken after a few uncomfortable moments when Oletta blurted, "Santa Claus!"

"No, it's Christmas Tree, you MORON!" replied the sentry and waved us by.

Down beyond the southern flank of a ridge, the sergeant found the MSR. In a mile or two, driving by the light of the moon, we turned off to the British encampment, where Oletta left me at the officers' mess tent, saying he would go over to their sergeants' mess and come back for me in about an hour. The camp was blacked out, of course, and when with unerring accuracy Oletta drove up to the officers' tent, we were challenged by a soldier standing in front of its heavy canvas outer door. Oletta explained our identities and a moment later a tall man who turned out to be the battalion commander emerged. "Sir," said the soldier, "we have a Yank leftenant." The tall man said, "Welcome, Yanks," and saluted us. When we had jumped from the jeep and properly returned his greetings, he said that he was on his way to the latrine but that I was to go in and introduce myself.

Inside the double canvas doors, a vestibule was lined with an assortment of field jackets, hats, and the like. After hanging my steel helmet and helmet liner on a peg, I entered an interior closed door that opened on the dining room, in which fifteen or twenty officers in casual uniform were being looked after by two sergeants in resplendent red jackets. Here, in my brief experience, was the ultimate expression of the romance of war. We were close to the Line, in fact barely out of enemy artillery range. No matter. Among battalion and company regalia on the canvas walls, a portrait of the queen looked down on tables covered with white linen and laid with silver and china, around which sat or stood the Brits talking and smoking and drinking Scotch whiskey. At my arrival, one of the officers came over to greet me. Because of my ignorance of

British insignias of rank, and because he most probably outranked me anyway, I said, "Lieutenant Jack Campbell, Sir, U.S. Eighth Army."

"A Yank, and a bloody Campbell to boot,"[4] came a burred quip from one of them, followed by laughter and handshaking around.

It was a warm reception interrupted momentarily when one of them advised me cheerfully that it was customary for officers not to wear their sidearms in the mess room, advice that invoked more laughter. I hung my web belt and pistol beside my helmet. And until Sergeant Oletta came for me, we smoked, drank, were served dinner, and talked quite properly of anything but the war.

Between tours of the Line, I was given duties in and near Seoul, assignments that allowed the seven of us, coming in from various directions, to see the sights of the city and relax in our home billet, which as it happened was closer to the war than we supposed it to be. Given clear weather and moonlit nights, the North Koreans were in the habit of sending down strange little airplanes to bomb targets in or near Seoul. Biwinged, covered with fabric rather than metal, powered by a single one hundred–horsepower engine, and crewed by a pilot and a gunner, each plane carried two of what we were told were fifty-pound bombs, one under each of its lower wings. The official international designation for this strange craft was Po-2, the *Po* standing for Polikarpov, thus betraying its Soviet origins. In Korea, it was known universally among Allied troops as "Bedcheck Charlie" and looked like something from the First World War.

Flying by moonlight and hugging canyon floors, the little bombers sneaked under our radar net to find targets they hoped to blow up or set on fire. Their ambition apparently did not extend much further than making an irksome nuisance of themselves. But on the night of June 16, the first night we newcomers were to see them, they accomplished that and more. The morning after our arrival at Fifth Advance, we had been told of the Bedcheck Charlies and that, if we happened to be in residence when the moon was up, we could expect to be awakened in the middle of the night by air raid sirens. The sirens meant, if for no other reason than the dangers posed by the windows of our high-ceilinged rooms, we were to get out of the hospital immediately.

Each room had two tall windows that together took up most of the outer wall. Of a slightly green cast, speckled with bubbles or other imperfections, they were pleasing artifacts of the hospital's early history but in a bombing attack their flying shards would be deadly. Our mentors said that so far "we" had not been bombed, but for all anyone knew we could be next on the list. On the 16th of June, in the middle of the night, the sirens shrieked and the lights went out. The unholy sirens were in one way or another synchronized with a master switch that turned off every light in both the air force and army compounds, leaving us to flounder around in the black halls until we found an outer door. Once out, several of us scattered into a small grove of pines in the backyard, over which in the next moment floated two Bedcheck Charlies. They seemed to float because they flew so slowly and, until they were on top of us, the noise of their engines was drowned by the sirens.

It was surreal. The two little planes in tandem and plain as day in the moonlight were like giant owls, possibly two hundred feet off the ground and chugging along at what seemed to be about fifty miles per hour, but which we learned was more like eighty-five. They left us alone. Their target that night was the immense U.S. fuel dump at Kimpo Air Base near Inchon on the other side of Seoul. They, and others like them who had approached by different routes, set fire to the dump in what was to be one of the most spectacular, if hardly the most deadly, combat operations of the war.

As reported by Corporal Jim Morrissey (1953) in the June 18 issue of *Pacific Stars and Stripes,* their total bag in the one-million-gallon fire amounted to four dead and twenty wounded Korean civilians hit by two stray bombs that missed the dump and fell in a residential part of Inchon, as well as sixteen wounded American firefighters, only three of whom required hospitalization. These casualties, when compared with the rest of the Korean War dead and wounded, counted for next to nothing. But the little bombers were nevertheless a nasty thorn in our side. Their war on the nerves of the UN troops and South Korean civilians was one of the best of the many and varied Korean psywar attempts produced by the enemy side. If we were to have taken a dispassionate view—which no one did—of Allied efforts to shoot down the Bedcheck Charlies, the whole thing would have seemed like a comic opera. The technological sophistication of mid-twentieth-century America and her allies to the contrary, we simply could not get at the peculiar little planes. In another column in the same issue of *Pacific Stars and Stripes,* Warren Franklin (1953), a civilian writer, gives the reasons for this embarrassing failure as enumerated by an air force source:

1. The Red planes skim over the Korean hills and up the narrow valleys beneath the United Nations radar screen.
2. Searchlights and antiaircraft defenses are manually and mechanically controlled. There are little or no radar-controlled antiaircraft guns necessary for night aerial defense.
3. The jet all-weather night fighters are virtually "helpless" against the 100 mile an hour enemy planes because of their [the jets'] tremendous speed, split second maneuverability, and great range of turn.

4. American trainer-type light planes which could successfully maneuver against the Red bombers are not equipped with the necessary radar equipment to find and track them in the dark.

As the exploding dump turned much of the western sky a fiery red, our sirens were turned off and we collected ourselves. Three of us climbed a narrow interior stairway to the hospital roof where, with a pair of shared binoculars, we had a grandstand view of the inferno. The spectacle included reflections of our searchlights on the smoke column, "rockets" (flaming fifty-gallon fuel barrels), and a few small aircraft possibly including the Red planes. We did not learn how many, if any, of the bombers were shot down on that or on other nights. Rumor went around that in that same raid a U.S. pilot in a Corsair (the famous marine corps "gull-winged," propeller-driven fighter of the Second World War) closed on a Bedcheck Charlie, but he was flying so fast, relatively speaking, that he crashed into the enemy plane, killing both pilots. The rumor included that the American pilot's last radio message was simply, "Shit!"

The senior officer and overall boss of our hospital billet was a spare, severe air force lieutenant colonel. A high-ranking barracks master-at-arms, he had a gravelly voice and seldom smiled, and we knew very little about him. Two or three nights after the Kimpo fire, two of the little biwings came again down the canyon, nearly brushing the tops of the pines with their wings. A few moments later, when we heard the loud *crump, crump* of their bombs, this time close by in downtown Seoul, the three of us scrambled back to our perch. But we were barely settled when a disembodied head appeared through a hole in the roof and an unmistakable gravelly voice said, "Get the hell down off of here!"

After those two nights of their flying over our backyard we did not see the bombers again, but as long as they had moonlight, they prowled around our bailiwick setting off the air raid sirens, which in turn set off what had become a standard response from the nearest officers' club. Behind our billet in the old hospital was a small building of mortared stone, which we were told had been a Shinto shrine during the Japanese occupation but was now the club. Such are the fruits of war—in this case largely because so soon after the end of World War II neither we nor the Koreans were especially fond of the Japanese. Outside and against one end of the building was what passed for an air raid shelter. A roofless rectangle, it was made of one wall that was the stone end of the shrine and three other walls of sandbags laid up to shoulder height, and furnished with a narrow, blind opening. It was the kind of hideout that if its occupants kept their heads down, would give reasonable protection from a fifty-pound bomb, providing of course that the bomb landed *outside*, not *inside*, the shelter.

The bombers usually came late at night. To avoid being routed out of bed, we learned from the club's more permanent members to drink and play poker until the sirens sounded and the lights went out. Then, carrying our drinks, we would make our way to the air raid shelter. In anticipation of the impending blackout, we were taught to have two drinks handy. One drink was for the road, and once the few dozen of us had gotten inside the shelter, we drank our second in unison. Then, according to club custom, we smashed the empty glasses against the stone wall and sang the "Dinghy" song, an uncomplicated ditty of a single stanza that went:

> Dingaling, oh dingaling
> Blow it out your Ass!
> Bombs away are coming
> Bye and bye

This was the signal that the club was closed for the rest of the evening.

As usual I got in some birding, although because we had arrived late in the breeding season, many species were lying low on their nests and some, perhaps, had deserted the war-torn countryside. One evening, however, and up on the Line of all the unlikely places, I heard a so-called common cuckoo. In Eurasia it is the most widespread of its tribe, but in the Americas its unmistakable call is made only by cuckoo clocks. In theory, my best chance to see "new" birds was at the Queen's Palace, the ancestral home of Korean royalty. The expansive grounds on the outskirts of Seoul were dotted with ponds upon which dwelled wild ducks and herons and other fascinating birds. But they dwelled in happy seclusion because by the time I got there the whole grand estate was under lock and key. Its high perimeter fence topped with barbed wire and plastered with "Keep Out" signs had resulted from the imaginative souvenir hunting of an American GI who, during one of the battles for Seoul, had lifted from the palace a treasured rug made of leopard skins. Somehow he had managed to ship it home to the States where his relatives had his hometown paper take its picture. The picture was seen by the army, who then sent it back to the South Koreans, who then locked it up in the Queen's Palace for good.

I had better luck, in two quite different ways, with the plovers and terns nesting among the dunes that rolled back from the left bank of the Han River below the U.S. Army Corps of Engineers' bridge that had replaced those destroyed in the fighting. Here, on the edge of Seoul, the Han's channel ran against the right bank. Dunes of light gray sand, among which the Kentish

Ruins in Seoul, June 1953 (photo by author)

plovers and little terns laid their eggs, reached back from the opposite shore for an eighth of a mile, nearly as far as one of the runways of K-16.

Two trails led through the dunes from the river's edge to the open country around K-16. On the two days in which I chased around among the dunes, taking pictures of nests and making drawings of the parent birds, poor women and children walked the sandy tracks on their way to and from washing their clothes in the river. Watching me with a certain wary curiosity, they stuck closely to the trails, ignoring the crying birds flying up from their nearby nests. I wondered why these destitute survivors of the battles for Seoul did not gather the perfectly edible and nutritious eggs. As a fledgling anthropologist, I theorized that they left the eggs alone because of some traditional respect for, or fear of, plovers and terns, but I was advised afterward by an Eighth Army captain, himself a birdwatcher, that the most probable reason for their not taking the eggs was that the surrounding dunes were strewn still with land mines.

Much of Seoul lay in ruins, the result of the battles of 1950 and 1951. Some of the city had been spared, including the cloistered grounds of the Queen's Place, as well as most of the locality now occupied by Eighth Army and Fifth Air Force headquarters. Yet in the center of Seoul, many of the old two-story or taller buildings made of mortared brick remained as heaps of rubble facing on streets cleared by the U.S. Army Corps of Engineers. Thousands of the city's population had been killed or displaced by the fighting. In the spring of 1953, orphaned children, roaming alone or in small bands, survived as best they could among the ruins. They were in no danger of outright starvation. Handouts of army rations from American and other UN soldiers assured that, and they had managed to find shelter of sorts. However, they were malnourished and dressed in rags. Being so small and unattended, they were in danger of literally murdering one another. For several months a Roman Catholic relief group had been hard at work rounding up the waifs—many of whom did not like being rounded up—and taking them off to civilized care. When we were there, quite a few were still running wild as March hares.

Meanwhile, enterprising Korean merchants who had survived the destruction were back in business. They set up shop in makeshift kiosks of salvaged bricks and lumber built on the sidewalks in front of what was left of the buildings' facades or in cave-like storefronts hollowed from the rubble-filled street-level rooms. They sold an array of small goods, the most noticeable being homemade brass souvenirs, shopworn sundries, and contraband antibiotics. The sundries and drugs were for Korean civilians; the brass souvenirs were meant for the GI trade. These, the products of a thriving cottage industry made possible by the war, consisted of a remarkable assortment of hundreds of ornaments, nearly all of them bowls or vases, fashioned from empty artillery and mortar shells.

Festooned with clusters of brass grapes and grape leaves, their lack of elegance was alleviated by the obvious skills of their artisans. My only purchase was an artillery or mortar shell lock, but after several decades of my associations with culture history museums, I hope that some far-sighted curator has put together a collection of the bowls and vases. Examples of a singular war-inspired folk art, their collective diameters must have reflected those of the breech bores of nearly all heavy weapons on both sides of the war. My lock, made for the hasp of a trunk or footlocker, is an impressionistic leaping carp, scales and all. It opens with a peculiar copper key hammered, I would guess, from a piece of stolen telegraph wire.

In one of the ruined buildings I missed my chance to have taken home an exceptional example or two of ancient Oriental art. The storefront's proprietor was a small, middle-aged Korean who spoke broken but understandable English and whose wares were the usual sundries and brass artifacts. As I was leaving, he noticed that I was an American lieutenant—in fact, by then I was wearing silver rather than gold bars.[5] This rank implied money and he said that he wanted to show me "very valuable things."

In the back of the room, a door of recently milled pine boards opened into a narrow passage that had been bored into the rubble and shored, walls and ceiling, with similar boards and studs. Similar to a horizontal mine shaft, the passage was fifteen or twenty feet long and ended in another door that was closed and secured with a padlock. As the man motioned me to follow, I made a point of opening the flap of my pistol holster. Because of the dangers of Fifth Column assassins and saboteurs, every UN soldier carried his weapon when on the streets of Seoul. Depending on rank or preference, the weapon of choice was usually a carbine, pistol, or revolver, and I wonder now why I did not back out then and there.

The small man, possibly noticing my hesitation, said, "Don't worry, no danger." After he had unlocked the inner door, we entered a square little room no larger than a typical middle-class American bathroom, which he lighted by pulling a string attached to a bare electric bulb overhead. The floor was stacked with a dozen or more boxes of various shapes and sizes, again made of freshly milled pine. Fitted with sliding lids, each contained a ceramic vessel of a lovely soft green color, wrapped in newsprint and unadorned except for lines of yellow metal that looked like gold and that filled one or a few irregular cracks in its surface. The Korean told me that the bowls and vases, of different sizes and shapes, had come from Chinese tombs north of the Yalu River. He said that long ago they had been mended with pure gold, and depending upon size he would sell them to me for from US$125 to US$300.

Neither in the Philippines nor in Japan or Korea were U.S. service personnel permitted to carry "American Green," an order intended to prevent a rampant black market in the universally popular U.S. currency. Instead we were paid in U.S. MPCs (Military Payment Certificates), which while not as dear as greenbacks, in the East Asian money business were the paper equivalent of the coin of the realm. What with combat pay and having been away from home base for going on two months, I was carrying something on the order of $600 in MCPs. Thus I could afford at least a couple of the vessels and would have had no trouble taking them back to Clark Field and the States. But I wondered if they were genuine, and because I knew nothing about Oriental art, ancient or otherwise, after he had unwrapped half of them I thanked him and turned him down.

A month later in Manila I looked up H. Otley Beyer, the famous expatriot American ethnographer and archaeologist who had been in the Philippines and elsewhere in East Asia since 1904. He was a small, impatient man in his seventies. Following the fall of the Philippines in early 1942, when the Japanese interned resident American civilians, he had avoided imprisonment because of his meeting with one Kano Tadao. A learned man who spoke

excellent English, Tadao had come down from Japan as a member of the commanding Japanese general's inner circle. While Beyer was anything but a col-
laborator, the two of them became intellectual friends.

I had been introduced to "Doc" Beyer soon after my reaching the
Philippines, and he had adopted me as sort of a pledge. He had taken an
equal liking to Sue, looking after her while I was in Korea. She had followed
me across the ocean on a Norwegian merchant ship, and now in Manila was
awaiting the imminent arrival of our first child, Donald MacIver. Doc Beyer
was a walking encyclopedia of East Asia lore, and in our first conversation
after my return from Korea I asked him about the bowls and vases. He
answered that they were of celadon mended with gold, that they derived
from the ancient Chinese Sung Dynasty (AD 960–1279). He said they were
not fakes and that if I were not so miserably ignorant I would have bought
as many as my MPCs allowed.

For my second and last assignment to the MLR, the same captain who
had entrusted me to the care of Sergeant Oletta now handed me to an army
lieutenant whose name was Bill Ross. The captain said that for the next few
days Ross would be showing me something of the western sectors of the
Line. Because of similar interests in such matters as shooting and fishing and
because of our having essentially the same rank (he was a second lieutenant
and, as I have noted, I had recently been promoted to "first"), our acquain-
tanceship was more casual than that I had had with Sergeant Oletta.

With Bill Ross driving the jeep and our reporting back to Eye Corps each
night, most of our four days of travel was a fascinating Cook's tour of the
battle line, up one ridge and down another. However, in the afternoon of our
first day on the back side of a ridge being held by a deployed U.S. infantry
company, we came upon a staff sergeant and a corporal. The corporal was
crying, and the sergeant was saying, "You did OK, kid. You did OK. Listen to
me!" The sobbing corporal, who looked as if he were all of eighteen years old,
was telling the sergeant how his patrol had been ambushed and how he had
to leave behind two of his five men. It had happened less than an hour before
and less than a mile away. Now, as an embarrassed voyeur, I was seeing war
without its romance.

Other adventures were less somber. We dropped in on two British infantry companies camped in the bottoms of narrow canyons. These men, while
lying in wait of possible enemy thrusts, had spent a week or two of hard
work decorating a nearby slope with painted stones in honor of the June 2
coronation of Queen Elizabeth. The stones were small boulders from the
beds of the canyons and had been painted red, white, and blue. They were
arranged to show a large, impressively good British crown accompanied in
large stone lettering by ELIZABETH REGINA.

Atomic cannon being hauled off the line, South Korea, 1953 (photo by author)

One day, as Allied observers, we watched a platoon of ROK infantrymen wearing freshly cut foliage on their helmets practice attacking another ROK platoon in a wooded canyon. Another day, with a borrowed military police riot gun, we went looking for spectral pheasants that Ross had seen the week before in some abandoned rice paddies. Our third day out, on a heavily traveled dirt road behind the forward ridges, we found an exceptionally big, long-barreled field gun that had just been pulled down from the Line by an army tractor and a dozen U.S. artillerymen. Neither Bill nor I had seen another like it, nor did we know what it was meant for until an artillery captain explained that it was an atomic cannon. Its low-yield shells were designed to wreak havoc among enemy companies and battalions. He and his men had been trained in its operation, which was the reason why they were there. But, he said, orders had come down at the last minute to scrub the mission and get the cannon back to where it had come from.

As always we traveled by jeep, Ross driving both the MSR and the side roads like a madman while I pleaded with him to slow down. Our western-most destination was a South Korean intelligence squad holed up in a dug-out roofed with the usual pine logs covered with two feet of dirt. An open, narrow horizontal window hung with strips of camouflage cloth identical to the window in the broadcasting studio faced north toward "Chicom" (Chinese Communist) troops hidden on the back side of a barren hill at a range of about a mile and a half.

To reach the dugout we first topped a ridge posted with the familiar "Moe is Watching You" sign, then drove down and out of a broad gully to stop beside a weapons carrier parked one hundred yards short of the top of the ridge. Just beyond was the bunker's single back entrance. The bunker was manned by a dozen ROKs commanded by a South Korean lieutenant who began telling us what they were up to in the way of collecting intelligence, but who was interrupted by an enemy shell that exploded just behind us. Cool as a cucumber, the Korean lieutenant said that under cover of darkness the night before, one of our M26 Pershing tanks had dug in to the left of us facing the Chinese hill, with the idea of using its 90mm (slightly more than 3.5-inch) gun as a stationary artillery piece.

He confessed that while he did not know what was going on, he supposed the Chinese were out to get the tank rather than our camouflaged bunker, but they had not got the range. He said this accounted for the wide misses of the incoming shells, because for the next thirty minutes we were under a continuous barrage. Fired from Chicom mortars beyond the crest of the hill in front of us,[6] the shells fell all around us, exploding with ear-shattering noise. Some of them were close enough to cause streams of dirt, like poured sugar, to sift down between the logs in our ceiling. A day later we were told that the barrage was of 120mm (4.75-inch) shells, fired from the largest mortar used by either side in the Korean War.

Neither the bunker nor the tank was hit. The tank, we learned later, pulled out soon after dark that night for more healthful terrain. Nevertheless, the barrage was nerve-racking, and after half an hour of continuous bombardment, Ross and I suggested that we would just as soon make a run for it. The Korean officer replied that while it was up to us, we took our chances either way; the bunker could not survive a direct hit, but on the other hand, if one of the big shells fell close to our departing jeep, it would likely kill us. We elected to bolt. Dashing out the back, we leaped into the jeep and drove at breakneck speed down and across the gully. For once, as Bill Ross reminded me later, I did not complain about his fast driving. The distance from the bunker across the gully and up the far side to where the Moe sign was posted was perhaps a mile. Except at the ridge crest, we were out of sight of the Chinese, but near the bottom of the gully about half way between the bunker and the Moe sign the road behind us was hit squarely by mortar shells. I was looking back at the time, and thought I saw either three or four of them hit simultaneously, but with smaller explosions than those from the shells raining down around the bunker.

The half-hour in the bunker and the run in the jeep marked the only time in my Korean adventure I experienced honest personal combat, as one-sided as it was. But there was a deadly sequel to the episode. As the heavy mortar barrage stretched on after our having got away, the ROK lieutenant gave his men the option of staying or getting out. The next day we were told that four or five of them had chosen to try escaping in the weapons carrier and were killed by a direct hit, apparently at the same place in the gully where the dirt track behind us had been ploughed by the smaller caliber shells. We never learned whether it was coincidence that the shells landed in that particular place or whether the Chinese had an observer who, lying low in the scrub above the road, had called in the coordinates.

My final assignments involved my reporting to army or air force officers at three locations in the vicinity of Seoul, the first of which was to an out-of-the-way compound to get practice in interrogating enemy prisoners. The prisoners were Chicom private soldiers who had recently been captured. They were being held in a small stockade of four or five acres enclosed by a high, woven-wire fence topped with concertina barbed wire. I was met at the gate by a sergeant who took me inside to one of the several one-story prefab buildings where I was introduced to the CO, a captain who, with a lieuten-ant, briefed me on what I was to do. I was not expected to ask the prisoners the usual battlefield questions concerning the names of their officers, the names and strengths of their fighting units, and other such urgent details. Those questions had been put to them soon after they had been caught. Rather, the two officers said that my principal task was to ask them—through an interpreter, of course—about their knowledge of and reactions to our psy-war efforts. Had they heard our broadcasts or seen our surrender leaflets? If they had, what did they think of them? Further, I was instructed to enquire what they knew of world events: geography, geopolitics (apropos of the cur-riculum at the Georgetown Foreign Service School), and major international political and military figures.

At the end of my fairly lengthy briefing I was surprised to learn that while this assignment was billed as practice, I was to do the practicing on my own. I would be closeted with one prisoner at time, plus the indispensable inter-preter, a Chinese Nationalist. Each interview was to take about an hour. The prisoners were brought in separately each in turn. Their faces were distinctive. Beyond that, they were of the same medium stature, low voice, and subservi-ent hangdog manner. They wore identical ragged uniforms of padded cotton. It was impossible not to feel sorry for them, and my feelings were reflected in the ways they were treated by the U.S. officers and enlisted men who guarded them. There was no shouting of orders, pushing, or shoving. Their captors felt sorry for them too.

I had been advised by the two officers that I would find the prisoners to be remarkably unhappy and that their misery was derived from their having been convinced by their own officers that if we were to catch them we would kill them. Even though in their few days of captivity they had been fed and treated very well, they still more or less expected to be shot at our earliest convenience. By way of helping to alleviate their fear of this terrible prospect, I was told to offer each of them a package of American cigarettes, which in the Far East during the war were nearly as dear as our MPCs. After the door was closed, we lit up all around, the prisoner from his own gratefully accepted pack. Then the three of us settled in for the interrogation. Not far into each of the interviews the Camels and my sunny disposition seemed to produce a certain thaw that resulted, I thought, in an honest attempt to answer my questions truthfully.

Unless the prisoners were consummate liars, which was possible, I soon learned that they knew nothing at all of our psywar efforts. They had been ordered not to pick up or read our leaflets, none of which they had even seen. Nor had they heard any of our friendly frontline broadcasts. Going on to other less relevant, yet nonetheless revealing spheres of interest, I learned that they were both illiterate and monumentally ignorant of the world beyond their peasant roots and their military service.

They had been exposed to lectures on geopolitics by political officers who had left out the geography. A reasonably large map of the world hung on one wall of the small room. To use one prisoner as a typical example, I pointed first to Africa and then to South America and asked him to give me the Chinese names for them. Silence. Closer to home, I asked him to point out the locations of Japan and the Philippines. Still no luck. Finally I asked him to show me England and the United States. He could not do this either, but cheerfully told the interpreter that England and the United States were close together. "How close?" I asked, "As close together as China and North Korea?" He replied that yes, they probably were.

As for famous men, they knew that Mao Zedong (Mao Tse-tung) was the Red Chinese chairman. They recognized the names of Stalin and Truman, but knew little about them or about other world figures. However, to my astonishment, one prisoner volunteered out of the blue that "Abraham Lincoln was a great man because he was the friend of the people." At the war's end the Chicom prisoners (many of whom had been forced into service) were given the option of refusing to return to Communist-controlled China. We could only hope that those choosing to return would not face retaliation for surrendering in the first place.

Chapter Five

The Leaflet Campaign

"Korea's Bloodless Battle," as it has been called by Eddie Deerfield (2002), the U.S. Army first lieutenant in command of a ten-man loud-speaker detachment in Pusan in 1951 and 1952, had its beginning less than twenty-four hours after President Harry Truman's announcement on June 30, 1950, that the United States was committed to a ground war in Korea.[1] The bloodless battle was launched when modified U.S. Air Force C-46 cargo planes, aircraft much like the C-47 noted in chapter 4, dropped 12 million leaflets, the largest one-day drop of the war, on South Korean (ROK) army troops and civilians.

Composed in Tokyo in typescript by the U.S. Eighth Army Psychological Warfare Section, and with the UN logo as its only illustration, this first message urged soldiers and civilians alike to "stand firm" and that help from the Free World forces was on its way.

As an anonymous amateur historian once remarked, psychological warfare has been around since Adam and Eve, but as a modern weapon of military combat its history goes back to the First World War of 1914–18, when the development of radio and aircraft and the increasing sophistication of mass printing techniques allowed for delivering both radio and leaflet messages to the fields of battle. These two media were to become combat standard in all subsequent wars that have involved large numbers of soldiers. In the Second World War and in Korea, while radio and loudspeakers served an impressive combat role, leaflets were the primary psychological warfare weapon.

Not counting the above-noted one-day 12-million-leaflet drop on friendly South Korean soldiers and civilians, nor its follow-up bombardment whose leaflets carried, in addition to essentially the same message as those of the first day, a photograph of General of the Army Douglas MacArthur and his generals, by the end of the Korean War UN forces had dropped or fired more than 2.5 *billion* leaflets on enemy troops and civilians.

Throughout the war all U.S. psychological warfare operations were under the control of the U.S. Eighth Army Far East Command in Tokyo. With the Korea exception described below, all UN leaflets were produced by the Eighth Army in Tokyo or elsewhere in Japan. In January 1951 with the escalation of the war, the Tokyo-based Eighth Army psywar section was elevated to division status and commanded by Brigadier General Robert A. McClure, a seasoned expert who had been director of psychological warfare at Supreme Headquarters, Allied Expedition Forces in Europe during the Second World War.

As I will relate further in regard to the operations of the First Loudspeaker and Leaflet Company ("L and L Company") from which I was taking lessons in the spring of 1953, leaflet production derived from both general and specific needs including requests from field commanders or intelligence officers regarding what particular leaflets or types of leaflets were needed for specific battlefield opportunities. Typically, such requests were transmitted immediately to Tokyo via radio-telephone, where the appropriate leaflets were taken out of stock (standby leaflet collections containing a variety of themes) or were created on the spot by a group of army experts whose ranks included intelligence analysts, language consultants, designers, and, above all, highly skilled writers and illustrators. Depending upon the urgency of a particular field request, this required working long hours after which their efforts had to meet the approval of Psychological Warfare Section officers. If approved, proofs were sent off under armed guard to Eighth Army's Third Reproduction Company based in the Japanese town of Motosumiyoshi, which lay not far from Tokyo in the direction of the naval port of Yokohama. At Motosumiyoshi members of the "Third Repro" (Reproduction) Squadron made the necessary plates and accomplished the printing of the leaflets, which were then sent off to U.S. air bases in Japan or to K-14 Air Base at Kimpo near Seoul (see map on page xiv) where they were loaded for drops in U.S. Air Force planes. USAF personnel were also responsible for loading and fusing the bombs.

In addition to those relatively few leaflets fired in artillery shells (see below), aerial leaflet delivery was accomplished by several aircraft including the big B-29s. This plane carried thirty-two 175-pound leaflet bombs containing a total of a million and a half 4 x 5–inch leaflets. The plane also carried larger bombs, each of which weighed 225 pounds when fully loaded and

Leaflet packets with fuse attachments ready for drop, North Korea, 1953 (courtesy of Paul A. Wolfgeher)

which carried 30,000 5½ x 8½–inch leaflets. Each bomb of this type was so designed that when it exploded, its outer shell dropped away and the compartments opened, scattering the leaflets in all directions. Typically dropped from 25,000 feet to effectively distribute the leaflets, a small explosive device on each bomb was set to detonate at a particular predetermined distance above the ground surface.

Other aircraft utilized were the Douglas C-47, Curtiss C-46 Commando, and Douglas A-26 Invader medium bomber, all of which flew at lower speeds and altitudes than the B-29s. Operating typically at 25,000 feet, the B-29s were out of reach of enemy ground fire while the lower, slower aircraft, which were unarmored and unarmed, were vulnerable to antiaircraft fire as they came over enemy territory. Occasionally the low-flying C-47s, C-46s, and A-26s were shot down by enemy antiaircraft guns, as the enemy jet fighters increasingly stuck to more northern skies. Because of the hazardous nature of this duty, after several missions each crew member of the low-flying planes was awarded a well-earned Air Medal.

The techniques employed to disperse the leaflets ranged from kicking wrapped bundles out of aircraft cargo bays to loading leaflets into 105mm or 155mm artillery howitzers. The British QF (Quick Firing) twenty-five-pounder

Soldiers loading leaflets in 105mm artillery rounds, place and date unidentified (courtesy of Paul A. Wolfgeher)

was the main artillery gun used by the British infantry and armored divisions during the Second World War, and in Korea it proved to have the most accurate delivery system of all the guns used. With a bore of 87.6mm (3.45 inches), it fired a standard twenty-five-pound high explosive shell but could also fire smoke, star, flare, and chemical shells of which its smoke and chemical shells could also be reloaded with leaflets.

As noted, U.S. forces used both 105mm and 155mm howitzers as leaflet artillery. The 155mm leaflet shell had a range of more than ten miles and carried 2,000 leaflets in rolls of 500 each, the leaflets separating from the shell in flight. These firings were usually carried out at dawn or dusk, twenty-five rounds at a time, into 500 x 500–yard areas having enough cover to enable enemy soldiers to retrieve leaflets without being seen by their officers.

Still, the primary means of delivery was to airdrop packages of leaflets, wrapped in heavy paper, on which a blasting cap and fuse were attached. These were shoveled, kicked, or thrown from the C-47s and the other low-flying planes. When the caps exploded, the bundles broke open, dispersing the leaflets.

THE UNITED STATES LEAFLETS

Plate 1

Psychological Warfare Division, G3 • Headquarters, EUSAK • APO 301 • Undated

The most common of all surrender leaflets aimed at us by the North Koreans was this 5 x 7–inch safe conduct pass, printed in blue, red, and yellow on white, which we "captured" in battle. The preservation of the Communist red star, peace doves, and typical leaf border transformed it into a UN certificate. Its back, in Korean and one line of Mandarin Chinese, follows closely the English message on its front.

주한 유엔군 사령부

신변안전보증서

김일성괴뢰군 장병들이여
쏘련놈들과 김일성 도당들에게 기만되여
악가운 목숨을 버리지말라 !

이 보증서를 가지꼬 유엔군 또는 대한
민국국군편으로 넘어오라 !!

이 보증서는 다음과같은것을 당신들에게 보장하
여주는 고귀한 증서이다 !!
1. 신변의 안전을 절대로 보장한다.
2. 충분한 식사와 주택을 보장하여준다.
3. 적당한 치료와 피복 및 일용필수품을 급여하며
   오락시설의 리용을 보장한다.

이 증명서는 한장으로 몇명이든지 사용할수있다

조국의통일과 평화를위하여 무기를놓고 유엔군
이나 대한민국국군편으로 넘어오라 !!!

이 보증서를 가지고오는사람에게는 신변을보호하며 우대할것이다
我軍. 對持證來的敵軍. 保證安全. 優待.
韓國地區聯合軍司令部

Plate 1
Back of flyer.

Plate 2

General Headquarters • Far East Command • Psychological Warfare Section • First Radio Broadcasting and Leaflet Group • APO 500 • 3 December 1951

This 3¾ x 5-inch safe conduct pass in red and black on buff has on its back an exact reproduction of a North Korean 100-Won note. On its front in three languages—Korean, English (directed at UN soldiers), and Chinese—it states that the certificate is a guarantee of safety to all desiring to cease fighting. Each statement is signed by General Matthew B. Ridgway, commander in chief, UN Command Forces. On both sides, running vertically, are the words "Your Safety is Guaranteed."

Plate 2
Back of flyer.

Plate 3

Psychological Warfare Division, G3 • Headquarters, EUSAK • APO 301 • 28 August 1952

This 5¼ x 10¾–inch leaflet printed in Korean in black on blue was requested specifically by Tenth Corps, U.S. Eighth Army, for the purpose of reminding North Korean soldiers of the relative ease of escaping to UN forces in rainstorms.

On its front it reads "A message to real Koreans" and "To true sons and daughters of Tangoon who have not accepted communism." Then, "The rains bring hardship, suffering, sickness, and death. . . . But they also bring. . . . the opportunity for which you may have been waiting."

The back contains a drawing of a disconsolate North Korean soldier sitting in the rain, and a message that "not for all North Koreans [but] only for those among you who have the good sense and courage to recognize what communism has done to your country."

「이」것은 인민군전체에 보내는 경고가
아니라 오로지 꽁산당이 북한을
망친것을 깨달을수 있는
능력과 용기를 가진 진정
한 이 나라를 딸에게
보내는 것이다。 오랫동안
꽁산독재를 벗어날 기회
를 기다리던 동지들은 이
것을 기억하라。

「동」지들이 다 아다싶이 비
온는 날 도망치기가 쉬운 것이
다。 그대들이 결심만 한다면
이것이야말로 둘도 없는 좋은
기회라는것을 알아야할것이다。
우리는 그대들을 기다리며 (환)
영할것이다。

Plate 3

Back of flyer.

Plate 4

Headquarters • Eighth United States Army • G3, Psychological Warfare Division •
APO 301 • 10 May 1953

Intelligence reports to the U.S. Eighth Army described the winter of 1952–53, and particularly the onset of its wet and muddy spring thaw, as being especially demoralizing to enemy troops in the field.

This 5 x 11–inch one-sided leaflet in Korean, printed in black, green, and brown on buff, compares life at home with life in a thawing MLR bunker. The captions reads "You Had a Happy Life Before the War" and "You are Leading a Miserable (Dog-Pig's) Life Now."

Plate 5
Psychological Warfare Division, G3 • Headquarters, EUSAK • APO 301 • Undated

In black and red on buff, this 5 x 6–inch "mute" leaflet was effective among both literate and illiterate NKPA troops. On its back, bold Korean characters in red read "ESCAPE! SAVE YOUR LIFE. COME OVER TO OUR SIDE." On its front a six-panel cartoon shows the joy of an NKPA soldier as he finds this safe conduct surrender pass.

Plate 5
Back of flyer.

Plate 6
Headquarters • Far East Command • Psychological Warfare Section
First Radio Broadcasting and Leaflet Group • APO 500 • 7 October 1952

A 7¾ x 10–inch leaflet in Chinese commemorating the founding of the United Nations on October 24, 1945.

On the front in full color are the flags of fifty-three member countries that support the war. The back, in addition to the blue and white UN flag, contains photographs in black on buff of the soldiers of seventeen UN nations who are in actual combat in Korea. Black and white captions in Chinese characters describe the roles in the conflict performed by the fifty-three participating countries, and in large print proclaims "UN—FOE OF COMMUNIST SLAVERY."

Plate 6
Back of flyer.

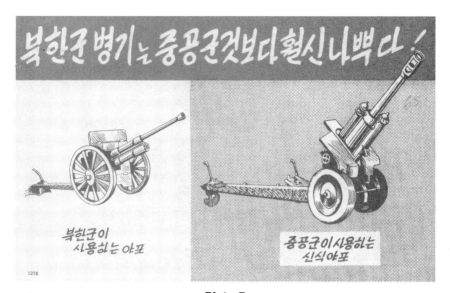

Plate 7
Headquarters • First Radio Broadcasting and Leaflet Group
8239th Army Unit • APO 500 • 2 February 1953

This leaflet was intended to foster Korean dislike of the Communist Chinese by furthering suspicion that the Chinese planned to take over North Korea. Measuring 5 x 8 inches and printed in Korean in red and black on buff, it is illustrated on its front with drawings of two field guns. One is a 76.2mm divisional gun labeled "The NKPA has this." The other is a modern 152mm howitzer labeled "The CCF has this," implying that the NKPA (North Korean People's Army) weapons are inferior.

On its back is a drawing of Mao eating rice labeled "Korea," and text reading "The CCF (Chinese Communist Forces) gives inferior weapons to the NKPA and keeps the best . . . for itself." It wants to "keep North Korea weak so China can swallow Korea like so much rice!"

Plate 7
Back of flyer.

Plate 8

Far East Command • First Radio Broadcasting and Leaflet Group
APO 500 • December 1952

Aimed at Chinese forces in Korea, the purpose of this 5 x 8–inch black on buff leaflet, based on a *Time* magazine cover, was to cause Mao to lose face because of his subservience to Stalin. The caption on its front reads "Beware of the Son Who Pays Tribute to the False Father." Its back illustrates a conversation between Father Stalin and Son Mao in which they describe how they will help one another. In the bottom panel Father Stalin says, "I will help you, little Mao, by sending thousands upon thousands of 'advisors' to supervise shipments of Chinese food and workers to Russia. They will teach you how to control China according to my wishes." Chinese prisoners of the U.S. Army commented that this leaflet missed its mark by showing Stalin and Mao without wearing their hats.

Plate 8
Back of flyer.

Plate 9

Psychological Warfare Division, G3 • Headquarters, EUSAK • APO 301 • 15 January 1953

A 5½ x 8–inch message printed in blue on buff in Chinese explains how CCF troops are being used as cannon fodder to promote Soviet aggression. The front shows Stalin pushing a terrified Mao at gunpoint into the muzzle of a UN cannon. In large Chinese characters, the caption proclaims "Soviet Russia is using Chinese as cannon fodder."

The back, with an illustration of a wounded soldier, carries a message to the effect that the UN has put forth honorable peace proposals, but that the "Communist Chieftains," urged on by Soviet Russia, have declined the peaceful settlement. The message ends with "Brothers: do not be cannon fodder for the Russians! Lay down your arms; we will be good friends."

蘇俄利用中國人當砲灰

共產黨眞會欺騙人、他們明明是替蘇俄主子執行侵略任務、却口口聲聲說「一切爲人民」。請看他們所作所爲、那一件不是在害人民！

聯軍抵抗侵略、保衛和平、提出光榮的停戰建議、共產黨受了蘇俄的指使、竟然拒絕和平！

聯軍武器優良、砲火强烈。共產黨逼着你們「死打硬拼」、這不是明明叫你們送死嗎？

弟兄們：不要替蘇俄當砲灰了！放下武器、我們都是好朋友。

8708

Plate 9
Back ot tlyer.

Plate 10

Headquarters • Far East Command • Psychological Warfare Section
First Radio Broadcasting and Leaflet Group • Tokyo • APO 500 • 23 June 1952

The U.S. Eighth Army produced leaflets for each of the UN member nations who contributed combat troops to the war. This 6 x 6–inch black, red, and blue on buff example in Chinese carries on its front a message explaining how Turkey has for many years resisted the threat of neighboring Russia and that now Turkish soldiers are in Korea to help halt Communist aggression in this part of the world.

On the back of the leaflet there is an invitation to Chinese soldiers to "Come over to our side to preserve your lives for the free days to come!" accompanied by photographs showing Turkish troops sharing conversation and cigarettes with their ROK friends.

中共官兵們：
土耳其是派
兵來韓參加
聯軍,抵抗共
產侵略的國
家之一.

土耳其士兵拿香
煙招待韓國战友.

土韓兩國兵士在
防地休息歡談.

6505*

Plate 10

Back of flyer.

Plate 11

Headquarters.• Far East Command • Psychological Warfare Section •
First Radio Broadcasting and Leaflet Group • 8239 AU, APO 500 • 12 July 1952

A two-sided 5 x 8–inch leaflet printed in black and red on buff is aimed at North Korean civilians for the purpose of impeding enemy troops and transports. On its front is a large caption in red that reads "WARNING" above a map showing military targets in red on North Korean highways and railroads. These targets are described as including Communist soldiers and equipment living or stored in "your houses," and exhorts the civilians to save their lives by leaving their homes "IMMEDIATELY" in anticipation of an imminent Allied attack.

1205

Plate 11

Back of flyer.

Plate 12
Headquarters • First Radio Broadcasting and Leaflet Group •
8239th ARMY UNIT • APO 500 • 11 March 1953

Printed in Korean in black and red on buff, this 5 x 5–inch leaflet is aimed at turning North Korean students against the Communist regime by raising their awareness of Communist suppression of free education. On its front is the students' ball and chain, the ball labeled "Political Training." Kim Il-sung is depicted as the teacher and the book he is pointing to is entitled "Russian Revolution." On the blackboard are stirring Russian maxims while on the floor lie confiscated books with titles such as "World Peace," "Democracy," "Human rights," etc. and a sign warning that anyone who touches these books "will be judged a reactionary."

On the back of the leaflet, under the heading of "The True Mission of a College Education" are listed four positive ideals to strive for in order to achieve freedom of development.

진정한 대학교육의 사명

1 학생의 사상을 수구적으로 제한하지 않고 이를 적극적으로 확대하도록 노력하는 것이다.

2 학생에게 일정한 주의만을 주입하지 않고 각종의 사상을 자유로 비판하도록 권면하는 것이다.

3 학생의 개성을 강제로 구속하지 않고 자유로 발전하도록 장구하는 것이다.

4 학생으로 하여금 형의노예가 되지말고 진리와 산노구가 되도록 함양하는 것이다.

가 북한학생에게 껜 학원의 자유가 보장되어 있는가?

Plate 12
Back of flyer.

황해도 농민들이여

쌀을 감추라!

공산당 때문에 굶지말라!

Plate 13
Far East Command • First Radio Broadcasting and Leaflet Group •
APO 500 • 25 October 1952

This 5 x 8–leaflet entitled "Hide Your Rice" depicts on its front a Korean farmer and his daughter (?) burying a large container of grain. Printed in Korean, in black on white with red lettering, it is designed to encourage farmers to withhold rice from Communist collectors. The text reads "Farmers . . . HIDE YOUR RICE! DON'T STARVE FOR COMMUNISTS!"

On its back are three panels, the first showing the completion of the burial of the grain: "Now they won't find our rice." In the second, the farmer points out an empty grain sack to the collector: "How can we pay the material tax without enough harvest? This is all we have." In the third panel the farmer gives grain to anti-Communist forces: "Anti-Communist patriots! Here is my humble contribution!"

Plate 13
Back of flyer.

Plate 14
Headquarters • First Radio Broadcasting and Leaflet Group •
8239th AU, APO 500 • 30 April 1953

In Chinese, this dramatic 5 x 8–inch leaflet printed in blue and black on white was designed to increase animosity toward a Russian-inspired marriage law that was resulting in suicides and forced marriages rather than emancipating Chinese women.

The illustration on its front shows a Chinese woman committing suicide by hanging, with the caption reading "The New Marriage Law . . . forces your women to death." A suicide note lies on the table.

The illustration on its back is equally poignant. Forced into marriage to a Communist cadre member, a young widow thinks of her former soldier/husband who died in Korea while their son cries for his father. The caption reads "Chinese soldiers! If you should die in Russia's war, your families will live in much more suffering."

Plate 14
Back of flyer.

Plate 15
Headquarters • United States Army Forces, Far East • First Radio Broadcasting
and Leaflet Group • 8239th ARMY UNIT, APO 500 • 19 January 1953

Printed in black on yellow, this 5 x 8–inch message in Korean is intended to create dissension between North Koreans and the CCF. The drawing on the leaflet's front is of a CCF soldier assaulting a Korean woman. The Korean characters on the right read "Save your wife and sisters from the evil hands of the Chinese Communists!"

On the back is a story told in cartoons of a Korean soldier who witnesses a CCF soldier trying to rape the wife of one of his comrades. According to UN intelligence sources, however, this theme was ineffective because of strict NK and Chinese policies regarding rape.

Plate 15

Back of flyer.

Plate 16

Headquarters • First Radio Broadcasting and Leaflet Group
8239th AU, APO 500 • 20 April 1953

The history of this 8 x 10–inch leaflet in blue and black on buff is described in detail in chapter 5. With the knowledge that the Russian-made MIG-15 aircraft was being flown in the Korean War by Soviet, North Korean, and Chinese pilots, the U.S. Far East Command offered a generous reward to the enemy pilot who would give us an intact example of this excellent fighter plane.

Printed separately in Chinese, Korean, and Russian (Cyrillic), and signed by General Mark W. Clark, commander in chief of the Far East Command, copies of this notice, explaining on front and back the terms of the reward, were scattered along the Yalu River and elsewhere in northernmost Korea by the U.S. Air Force.

On the front of the Russian version, US$100,000 (equal in 2009 to US$750,000) is offered to the first pilot to fly a MIG to one of our South Korean air bases. Included is a drawing of the sought-after aircraft and a photo of a Soviet bloc Polish officer who defected to Denmark in a MIG-15.

HEADQUARTERS
FAR EAST COMMAND
APO 500

СМЕЛЫМ ЛЁТЧИКАМ РЕАКТИВНЫХ САМОЛЁТОВ   20 апреля 1953 года

ПУТЬ К СВОБОДЕ

Товарищи лётчики! Дальневосточное Командование предлагает свою помощь всем смелым лётчикам, желающим освободиться от коммунистического ига и начать новую, лучшую жизнь, с должным почётом в свободном мире.

Дальневосточное Командование гарантирует вам убежище, защиту, человеческую заботу и внимание. Вам дана полная гарантия в том, что ваши имена останутся в тайне, если вы того пожелаете.

Товарищи лётчики! Ваш смелый шаг приведёт вас к свободе и даст вам возможность жить в дальнейшем без страха за своё благополучие. По мимо этого, своим героизмом и решительностью вы поможете другим, указав им путь к свободе.

Дальневосточное Командование вознаградит суммой в 50,000 американских долларов каждого лётчика, который приведёт к посадке в Южной Корее современный реактивный самолёт в боевой готовности. Первый лётчик совершивший посадку на таком самолёте получит в награду добавочную сумму в 50,000 американских долларов за свою смелость.

Ниже даны инструкции всем лётчикам желающим освободиться от коммунистического ига.

Летите к острову Хануренто (о. Пенген-то), который находится в 50 километрах к югу от острова Чото. От Хануренто (о. Пенген-то) направляйтесь к авиобазе Кимпо, всё время находясь на высоте 6100 метров. Начинайте спускаться над авиобазой Кимпо и подготовляйтесь к немедленной посадке. Самолёты ОН будут охранять вас всё время летя над хвостом вашего самолёта. Если плохая видимость не позволит вам самостоятельно совершить посадку на авиобазе Кимпо, то направляйтесь к Сеульскому району, и находясь на высоте 6100 метров спустите посадочные колёса. Один из самолётов ОН подлетит вплотную к вашему и летя рядом приведёт вас к безопасному месту посадки. При первом-же контакте с самолётом ОН, или в случае попытки одного из самолётов ОН атаковать вас, моментально спустите посадочные колёса и начните с силой качать крыльями вашего самолёта.

Свободный мир ждёт вашего прибытия.

Mark W. Clark

МАРК В.КЛАРК
Генерал Армии США
Главнокомандующий Вооружёнными Силами
на Дальнем Востоке.

5701

Plate 16
Back of letter.

THE CHINESE AND NORTH KOREAN LEAFLETS

Many POW's like to play chess.

Plate 17

The overall most common leaflets on both sides of the Korean War were safe conduct (surrender) messages of several varieties. This 2½ x 7½–inch black and red on buff safe conduct pass, printed in English, Chinese, and Korean, folds to the size of a typical American wallet card. Unfolded, one side contains the Communist dove of peace and a photo of three smiling American prisoners playing chess, and on the other it proclaims that "the BEARER, regardless of nationality or rank is to be treated with leniency and guaranteed: 1. Security of life. 2. Retention of all personal belongings. 3. Freedom from mistreatment or abuse [and] 4. Medical care of wounded or ill."

The names of Kim Il-sung, supreme commander, Korean People's Army, and Peng Teh-Hual, commander, Chinese People's Volunteers, are included.

"It is comforting to know that whether returned to us or not, he is in good hands," said this wife of a POW when she heard that her husband was captured.

CHRISTMAS WILL BE HAPPY IN THE FAMILY

WELCOME MAIL—*Mrs. Christine Brown reads one of two letters received from her husband, Lt. Col. Gerald Brown, who is a prisoner of war in Korea.*

The families of POWs are not in torment every moment. Their hearts are at ease. They know their dear ones are out of danger, are in good hands and well treated. They receive letters from them regularly, see their photos in the newspapers and hear their voices over the radio.

MOST IMPORTANT OF ALL, they know their dear ones will be repatriated right after the armistice is signed, while the other American GIs and the British, Turkish, Puerto Rican, Greek, Dutch, French soldiers who are still at the front will have to stay in Korea, keeping vigil with the bleak mountains until the U. S. Government makes up its mind to leave Korea to the Koreans.   156

Plate 18

A 5¼ x 7¾-inch black and buff Christmas message printed on one side only. At the top it quotes the wife of an American POW as saying that "it is comforting to know that whether returned to us or not, he is in good hands."

It reminds English-speaking UN soldiers that American families get letters "regularly" from their POW relatives and get to see their faces and hear their voices in newspapers and on radio.

Then it reminds other UN combat troops that they must stay on in Korea after American soldiers, including repatriated American prisoners, have returned home.

Plate 19

Intended to exploit American soldiers' complaints about the slowness of the U.S. Army's rotation system, this brown on buff one-sided leaflet shows a forlorn homecoming on the beach of an American city. To quote: "and so at last they came home, some without legs and arms, others on stretchers, still others securely nailed down in a box two by six. . . ." This message is accompanied at lower right with a warning of the dire hazards of "later" rotation.

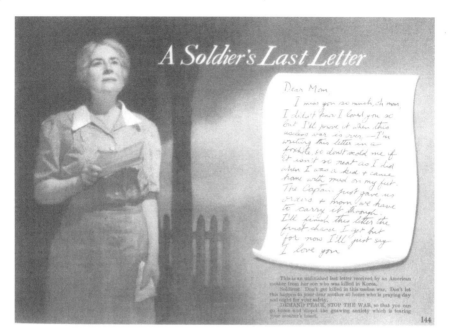

Plate 20

This enlargement of a one-sided 5¾ x 8–inch leaflet in full color testifies to the excellence of some of the Red Chinese composing and printing.

Entitled "A Soldier's Last Letter," it features an unfinished letter and a picture of a classic American mother whose anguish is described faithfully in the brief message at lower right that ends with "DEMAND PEACE, STOP THE WAR."

Plate 21

A 5¼ x 7¾–inch black on buff, this one-sided leaflet urges American combat soldiers, particularly those who are nearing rotation home, to keep their heads down and let their buddies do their fighting for them.

155A

Merry Christmas   Where there is

and

Happy New Year   PEACE

from   there is blessing.

The Korean People's Army
The Chinese People's Volunteers

KOREA 1952-3   (See inside)

Plate 22

This 3¼ x 4¼–inch three-color leaflet on white folds out to two 6½ x 8½–inch pages printed on both sides with a 700-word 1952 Christmas message from "The Korean People's Army" and "The Chinese People's Volunteers."

This well-written message explains further that the American government has been "stolen . . . by greedy big business!" and ends with "We offer you peace and friendship. America for Americans. Korea for the Koreans. China for the Chinese. Why should not we all, Korean soldiers, Chinese soldiers, American soldiers join our efforts for peace? . . . Then next Christmas, if not this one, can really be merry."

American Soldiers:

We are wishing you a Merry Christmas and a Happy New Year. We also have something to talk to you about.

Christmas is a day of peace and happiness. And a day for family reunions.

But this Christmas, for you, there is no peace. You are far away from those you love, in Korea, a country you never heard of three years ago—hundreds of thousands of casualties ago. Your family longs for you across the wide Pacific. Will they ever see you again? Will you ever see them?

You've been told you came here to stop "Communist aggression." But what do your own eyes and head tell you? The Koreans are fighting in their own country. The Chinese are defending their own nearby borders. Neither of these peoples ever dreamed of invading the United States. It is U.S. troops who have come here with bombs, napalm, germs and every other weapon of mass murder.

Bombs and guns can't break the spirit of the Koreans and Chinese, because they are guarding their homes. What about you? Is there any reason why you should be here instead of home with your folks? You are risking death or crippling wounds to hold one or two bare Korean mountains. What for?

The heartless men who sent you here have sent American soldiers to Europe. Those soldiers too are told that they must protect different countries from "Red aggression." But everywhere they go, they hear the people yelling, "Yanks, go home!" This wasn't the way the GI's were greeted everywhere in world War II, when they were really fighting against aggressors—the Nazis and Japanese warlords. Then they got

— 1 —

Plate 22
Page 1 of letter.

flowers. So something is wrong. What is it?

The truth is that American soldiers today are helping oppressors, not fighting them. You know how the Koreans "love" Syngman Rhee! You know how the Chinese "loved" Chiang Kai-shek whom they kicked out in spite of $6 billion worth of U.S. aid. In Japan the U.S. is letting convicted war criminals out of jail and giving them a new army to play with. In Germany, it's the same. In France, in Italy, they back governments which have sold out their own peoples for dollars, governments which order the police out every time working people strike for a living wage. Isn't this true? You know it is.

Why are Americans sent abroad to do this kind of dirty work, the exact opposite of every fine thing America ever stood for, in a way that would make Washington, Jefferson, Lincoln turn over in their graves if they knew it? Because the American government has been stolen from the American people by greedy Big Business which cares nothing about your life or anyone else's but only for its lousy profits. The corporations have made more money since the Korean war than they ever did before, out of arms orders for which the American people are paying through higher taxes, higher prices in every grocery store and the lives of their sons—YOUR lives. That's why the Brass Hats are throwing monkey wrenches into the talks at Panmunjom which could have succeeded a year ago. That's why they want more war everywhere, not peace.

Every people on earth is getting wise to this new kind of business— Murder for Profit. Americans at home are getting wise to it too. Millions are asking for peace and getting fed up with lies. American fathers and mothers have refused medals sent to them after their boys died in Korea. Hundreds of American pilots with decorations for courage in World War II have refused to fly in Korea. Tens of thousands of young men are dodging the draft. This is not because they are cowards. It is not because they

Plate 22
Page 2 of letter.

aretn't ptriotic. It's because they are beginning to understand that they've been fooled.

The patriotic thing is to fight for peace! The patriotic thing is to fight for friendship, not war, between peoples! What harm can peace do to any country, to America? What good does war bring to any nation, Americans included? The real traitors, the real criminals, are the few who send troops, thousands of miles away so they can rake in dollars. They think they own America, and for that matter the world. They think they own you. Who gave them the right? What kind of free American citizen are you when they can shove you into uniform, pack you in a boat, and send you to all ends of the earth for no other reason than this?

We, the Chinese People's Volunteers, are writing you this letter. We came here because, after we cleaned out the dirty grafter Chiang Kai-shek, you stormed into the land of our neighbor and threatened the first chance we ever had to build up our country. We don't want to fight anyone. We want to build in peace. We are in favour of peaceful coexistence and trade for every people in the world.

Don't believe the Big Money boys and politicians at home. They are no different from Chiang Kai-shek whom we ran out of China. Don't do what they want. Do what the people want.

We offer you peace and friendship. America for Americans. Korea for the Koreans. China for the Chinese. Why should not we all, Korean soldiers, Chinese soldiers, American soldiers join our efforts for peace? Then we don't need to be soldiers any more. Then next Christmas, if not this one, can really be merry. Then we can have a really Happy New Year in 1953! Let's make it so!

The Chinese People's Volunteers

Plate 22
Page 3 of letter.

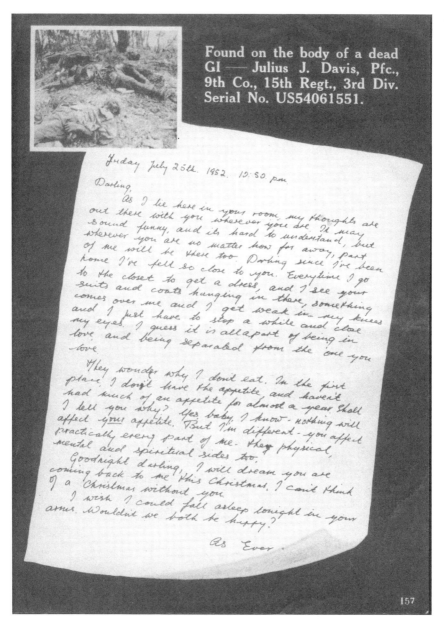

Found on the body of a dead GI — Julius J. Davis, Pfc., 9th Co., 15th Regt., 3rd Div. Serial No. US54061551.

Friday July 25th. 1952. 10:50 pm.

Darling,

As I lie here in your room, my thoughts are out there with you wherever you are. It may sound funny, and its hard to understand, but wherever you are no matter how far away, part of me will be there too. Darling since I've been home I've felt so close to you. Everytime I go to the closet to get a dress, and I see your suits and coats hanging in there, something comes over me and I get weak in my knees and I just have to stop a while and close my eyes. I guess it is all a part of being in love and being separated from the one you love.

They wonder why I don't eat. In the first place. I don't have the appetite, and haven't had much of an appetite for almost a year. Shall I tell you why? Yes baby, I know - nothing will affect your appetite. But I'm different - you affect practically every part of me - they physical, mental and spiritual sides too.

Goodnight darling, I will dream you are coming back to me this Christmas. I can't think of a Christmas without you.

I wish I could fall asleep tonight in your arms. Wouldn't we both be happy?

As Ever.

157

Plate 23

The white on black front of this 6 x 8–inch leaflet contains an impassioned love letter reputedly found on the body of an American private first class, and a small photo of dead soldiers on the battlefield. On its blue on white back an informal photographic portrait of a lonely young woman is accompanied by a quote from the letter: "Darling, I will dream that you are coming back to me this Christmas. I can't think of a Christmas without you."

Plate 23

Back of flyer.

Rotation or Runaround?

You're not getting closer to home but further away!

HERE'S THE RECORD

1951 April Rotation score adopted. Story is that all combat forces in Korea can go home after 6 months' service.

1951 Sept. Duration of combat duty in Korea goes up—from 6 months to 8 months.

1952 March New ruling says a man must have 36 points before rotation.

1952 Oct. General Clark raises "rotation score" from 36 to 38 points in face of manpower crisis.

1952 Oct. 21 Defense Secretary Lovett says "a man, regardless of the number of points he has accumulated, can come home only if there is a man there to replace him...." Some men have accumulated up to 44 points before rotation and the average has been about 40 points, Lovett reveals.

THAT'S FIVE TIMES THEY'VE SWITCHED THEIR PROMISES TO YOU, SOLDIER.

THINK YOU'LL EVER GET HOME, OR WILL YOU BE KILLED FIRST?

Plate 24

A 5¼ x 7½–inch leaflet of black and pink on buff. It and others of the same theme (see plates 19 and 21) exploited the loss of morale experienced by U.S. combat soldiers as military authorities increased incrementally the time required to serve before being "rotated" home. On its back are quoted the complaints of an American sergeant and two corporals.

Plate 25

Advising American frontline soldiers to hide out rather than fight was an often repeated theme. This 5 x 7–inch red on buff message on one side contains a poorly printed, indistinct drawing of dead soldiers lying on a battlefield, and on the other side, among other recommendations, advises the American soldier to "get in a hole and stay there."

USE YOUR HEAD, SOLDIER!

If You Want to Keep It!

Associated Press reported from Seoul, October 8:

> "North Korean artillery fired 39,000 rounds within 24 hours ending 6 o'clock October 7. Soldiers were pinned down for long hours in the trenches and bunkers by enemy fire which continued for days and nights."

Hanson Baldwin, *New York Times* military commentator wrote June 12:

> "Superiority on the battlefront, which the UN had a year ago, has now moved to the enemy side."

U.S. News & World Report wrote June 21:

> "U.S. air superiority in Korea is no longer absolute."

EVERY G.I. THAT'S BEEN IN BATTLE KNOWS THE SCORE:

- Bullets and shells hit everything above ground. He's smart to get in a hole and stay there.
- To go out on patrol is the best way to get killed. Don't do it.
- The first man forward in an assault is the first man to get hit. What's the good of looking for death?

USE YOUR HEAD AND PLAY SAFE!

167

Plate 25

Back of flyer.

Mr. Moneybags is in Florida this Christmas.

Where are you?   *In Korea!*

You risk your life, Big Business rakes in the dough.

傳單 —117

Plate 26

This 7 x 10–inch one-sided buff leaflet contains two photographs, the upper of which is in full color, while the lower is in purposefully contrasting black and white. As in plate 30, the aim is to remind the U.S. soldier that he suffers in combat for the sake of the war-mongering American wealthy class.

"PLEASE PRINT THIS"
Says Negro Preacher

The following letter was recently sent to a New York newspaper:

"As a Negro gospel preacher, formerly of New Orleans, La., I came to New York a few years ago as a victim of Jimcrow justice seeking freedom and equality.

I can't feel free, even here when such incidents happen as in Florida concerning the bombing of a Negro home, in which a Negro was killed and his wife has a 50-50 chance to live.

I understand Florida to be the playground of our civil-rights promising President. I noticed he intervened in the war in Korea, 5,000 miles from America, and ordered colored as well as white to go to slaughter people that never have done anything to this country.

But he will not intervene in such shameful cases as the electrocution of innocent Negroes and the recent bombing of a Florida home, and terrorizing action against the Jewish people as well. I know that the blood of many innocent Negro victims is crying out against this country.

The Bible tells me everybody must reap what they sow. This country can make all the A-bombs and H-bombs they want to, but according to the Bible this country must pay for the blood of these innocent people.

The Bible does not lie.
Please print this."

169

Plate 27

For the purpose of promoting further resentment of black soldiers toward the American white establishment, this 5¼ x 7½–inch one-sided leaflet of brown on buff is one of several messages that were directed at American black GIs and scattered by the millions on Korean battlefields during the course of the war.

LEST YOU FORGET!

Just one year ago, Christmas night 1951, **Mr. Harry T. Moore**, Negro leader of the Florida **NAACP**, was murdered by the Ku Klux Klan in his home in Mims, near Miami, Florida Klansman threw a bomb into the house. Mr. Moore was killed right away and his wife Harriet was badly wounded.

Mr. Moore had spoken out against Klan **terror** and lynchings against his people.

Between January 1950 and June 1951, **85 Negroes** have been lynched in the United States.

Decent white Americans are against these **crimes**, but the Attorney General, the police and politicians are too busy whipping up anti-Communist hysteria to spend time finding the criminals responsible, which they didn't do at other times either. They always have an' excuse.

NEGRO SOLDIERS! You've got a fight on your hands at home. Don't come fighting coloured people out here!

The only fight that makes sense is the fight for your own rights! The Koreans and Chinese are fighting against American aggression, they are fighting for their own rights too.

COME HOME FIGHT FOR OUR OWN RIGHTS.

166

Plate 28

This 5 x 7–inch black on buff leaflet, printed on one side only and directed at American black soldiers, is an example of some of the best enemy propaganda. Written with reason and restraint, it purportedly cites the number of recent Klan lynchings in the United States and states that "decent minded Americans" are against the brutality it describes. Then, speaking directly to the black troops, it proclaims "NEGRO SOLDIERS: You have a fight on your hands at home. Don't come fighting colored people out here!"

Plate 29

In an attempt to cause dissension among the two principal UN allies in the field, this 5 x 7½-inch black on buff leaflet from the North Korean Peoples Army (NKPA) is on one side addressed in bold letters to "OFFICERS AND MEN OF THE BRITISH ARMY" and contains a drawing and a photograph of two emaciated English babies and their distraught mothers.

On the other side are Truman (with fangs) and Churchill holding an American flag with a note to British soldiers telling them "DON'T DIE TO NO PURPOSE FOR THE YANKEES!!"

Plate 29

Back of flyer.

Why is the American ruling circle busily expanding armament, disregarding the hardship and misery of the people? It is because their only concern is war and war profits and not peace and peaceful construction.

12525

Plate 30

A 3¾ x 6–inch black on white leaflet that reports a devastating flood in South Dakota and Kansas and in addition reminds the American soldier that the "American ruling circle" is concerned only with war and war profits, not with the "hardship and misery of the people." The front shows an American "fat cat" receiving stacks of money from a cannon while the back contains a map of the U.S. storm area and a drawing of people and livestock being carried away in the flood.

Plate 30

Back of flyer.

Replies of Joseph V. Stalin

to Questions by James Reston, Diplomatic Correspondent of "New York Times" Received on December 21, 1952

Question: With the arrival of the New Year and the beginning of the new administration in the United States is it still your conviction that the Union of Soviet Socialist Republics and the United States can live peacefully in the coming years?

Answer: I still believe that war between the United States of America and the Soviet Union cannot be considered inevitable and that our countries can continue to live in peace.

Question: Wherein lie the sources of the present international tension in your judgement?

Answer: Everywhere and in everything wherever the aggressive actions of the policy of the "cold war" against the Soviet Union find expression.

Question: Would you welcome diplomatic conversations with representatives of the new Eisenhower administration looking towards the possibility of a meeting between yourself and General Eisenhower for easing world tensions?

Answer: I regard such a suggestion favourably.

Question: Would you co-operate in any new diplomatic approach designed to bring about an end to the Korean war?

Answer: I agree to co-operate since the U.S.S.R. is interested in ending the war in Korea.

130115

Plate 31

For the American combat soldier who was interested in the larger dimensions of the Korean conflict, this 5¼ x 8¾-inch one-sided black on buff leaflet distributed in combat in the winter of 1952–53 explains that Stalin himself wants to end the war. James Reston was an outspoken left-leaning critic of America's involvement in the Korean War.

General Nam Il Defines Basis For Armistice Talks

General Nam Il, chief delegate from the Korean People's Army General Headquarters, on July 10, in a brief speech, defined the basic attitude of the Chinese and the Korean peoples towards the negotiation for an armistice in Korea. He stated:

"Commander of the United Nations Forces General Ridgway on June 30 stated that he was willing to conduct negotiations for an armistice. My Supreme Commander Kim Il Sung and Commander Peng Teh-huai of the Chinese Volunteers, conforming with the hopes and desires of the peoples of Korea and China and all the peoples of the world, agreed to conduct negotiations with General Ridgway, and have sent me as a representative of the Korean People's Army to these negotiations. The Korean people have always held and still do, that the war in Korea should be ended quickly. Therefore, they agreed with enthusiasm to the proposal of Mr. Malik, Soviet representative in the United Nations, on June 23, that both belligerent parties negotiate for a cease-fire and an armistice, and that both parties withdraw their troops from the 38th Parallel.

We consider that in order to put an end to the Korean war, such important problems have to be solved as a cease-fire and the with-drawal of the troops of both sides from the 38th Parallel, as a basic condition for the realisation of a cessation of hostilities in Korea, and the withdrawal of foreign troops to ensure that the flames of war will not flare up again in Korea. Therefore, on behalf of the Korean People's Army, I make the following proposals:

1. On the basis of mutual agreement, both parties simultaneously order the cessation of hostile military actions of each and every sort; the army of each party stops its bombardment, blockade and recon-naisance against the other party; the navy of each party stops its bombardment, blockade and reconnaisance; and the airforce of each party stops its bombing and reconnaisance against the other party. Obviously, a cease-fire between the two parties not only can reduce loss of life and property, but is also the first step to put out the flames of war in Korea.

2. The 38th Parallel should be fixed as the military demarcation line from which the armed forces of both parties should simultaneously be withdrawn 10 kilometres. This should be done within a certain limit of time. The areas evacuated by both parties will be a non-military zone in which neither of the parties should station their armed forces or carry out any military action. The civil administration of those areas should be restored to the status quo ante June 25, 1950.

At the same time, talks should be conducted immediately on the exchange of prisoners of war, so that prisoners of war of various countries may return home quickly and join their families.

3. All foreign troops should be withdrawn in the shortest possible time. With the withdrawal of foreign troops, the ending of the Korean war and the peaceful settlement of the Korean question will be basically assured. The Korean people, the Chinese people, the Soviet people and the peace-loving people throughout the world, including the American and the British peoples, all ardently demand the early ter-mination of the Korean war and the peaceful settlement of the Korean question. I hope that we can reach an agreement in these negotiations in order to satisfy the demands of the broad masses of the people."

THE KOREAN PEOPLE'S ARMY
THE CHINESE PEOPLE'S VOLUNTEER FORCES

朝鮮人民軍首席代表南日將軍在停戰談判會議上發表的三項建議

Plate 32

A one-sided 5 x 7¾–inch black on buff leaflet that testifies to the sophistication of some of the CCF and perhaps NKPA writers. Aimed at thoughtful American soldiers, we assume that the general's speech reflects the views of the Chinese and North Korean hierarchy on what the armistice negotiations ought to accomplish, views that on paper at least are similar to those of the United Nations.

Gen. Nam Il

TRUTH WILL OUT!

WHY HARRISON AND CLARK BROKE OFF THE ARMISTICE TALKS?

Your General Clark and Harrison, his representative, have broken off the truce talks. American propaganda stories tell you this is because Gen. Nam Il turned down their latest offer on the exchange of POWs.

THIS IS NOT TRUE.

On October 8, Harrison walked out of the truce meeting and declared an indefinite recess without waiting to discuss Nam Il's very reasonable proposal. The Koreans and Chinese say:

"All prisoners should be sent home." U.S. POWs should be sent back to the States, Britishers to Britain, and the captured men from Turkey, Canada, France and other countries should be sent back each to their own homes to their folks. As to the Koreans and Chinese, needless to say, they can go to no other places than Korea and China.

Following out this principle, Gen. Nam Il made a new proposal. This stated:

William Harrison

"We accept your suggestion that the POWs on both sides should be sent to agreed places in the demilitarised zone. We suggest they should then be handed over to the control of the other side. Then, they should be interviewed and we accept your suggestion that Red Cross teams from both sides should interview the POWs. They should then be classified and repatriated according to nationality and original address, with inspection teams made up of neutral nations present as observers during the interviewing, classifying and repatriating of the prisoners."

Plate 33

This 5¼ x 7½–inch undated blue on buff Communist message does not identify its place of origin. Largely for fear of losing face, it repeats in detail the ongoing CCF-NKPA argument that at the conclusion of the Panmunjom peace talks all POWs must be returned to their own native countries. This CCF-NKPA fear was well-founded; when the armistice was eventually signed, a total of 359 UN troops refused repatriation, while 22,000 Communist soldiers refused.

This was so reasonable that Harrison was at a loss what to say. He must have had orders to find some excuse for breaking off the talks, so without discussing Nam Il's proposal, he slammed out of the conference tent.

Have you ever been told about this by your superior officers?

Obviously Harrison was ordered to break off the talks because the Pentagon wants the war to go on.

We ask you to think this over. More than 105,500 youth of the "United Nations" have become casualties between May and September this year. The ones responsible for their deaths or maiming are the men in the White House and the Pentagon who give the orders for wrecking the truce talks. Because the whole draft of the Armistice agreement was basically agreed by both sides as far back as May.

If the selfish men behind American policy today did not insist on keeping back the prisoners of war, there would have been an armistice in Korea months ago. And these 105,500 casualties would have been avoided.

The present breaking off of the truce talks is very dangerous. It will cost many more casualties among American youth.

IS IT WORTH IT?
IS IT RIGHT?

162

Plate 33
Back of flyer.

In contrast, beginning in the middle of 1952 when the MLR became more or less static along the North Korea–South Korea border and the battleground was North Korea, CCF (Chinese Communist Forces) and NKPA leaflets were increasingly delivered on foot. For want of suitable aircraft, their mechanized means of getting leaflets to UN troops were limited to accurate but short-range mortars and longer-range field guns such as those shown in plate 7. More commonly, foot soldiers carried in their backpacks bundles of leaflets that they scattered on the battlefield or sometimes hung as gifts on the barbed wire of no-man's-land; the example shown in plate 22 came in a yellow fiber "stocking" as a Christmas present. And in addition to infantrymen, the Chinese forces in North Korea sent North Korean women and children across the battle line carrying satchels of leaflets to scatter along the way.

No-man's-land trails, during this static period when the armistice talks at Panmunjom dragged on, were used both by UN and by CCF and NKPA patrols. A large percentage of the enemy leaflets picked up in combat by UN soldiers were found along these informal routes of travel and the most curious of Korean War techniques for delivering printed propaganda were the peace post boxes installed along these same trails by the NKPA. The boxes held friendly messages in English that invited UN patrols to reply in kind, the idea being that the exchange would produce gossip that the North Koreans could use to their propaganda advantage.

For my first lessons in the practical applications of the leaflet war I was told to get out of my field clothes and combat boots and back into Class A air force blues and shiny black shoes. It was a metamorphosis demanded by Fifth Air Force Advance, whose brass had decided that it was high time I got back to looking like an air force lieutenant. Later I imagined that this order of dress was prompted by ARCS, who were sending up from Clark a contingent of 581st leaflet people to help Eighth Army install a new leaflet producing press, and that I was to be an advance ambassador. With a corporal as driver and guide, on a bright blue-sky morning I was introduced to the Eighth Army First Loudspeaker and Leaflet Company, Army Post Office (APO) 301,[2] the only UN unit in Korea that was producing propaganda leaflets.

Our way led down a dusty road on the southern outskirts of Seoul to the First L and L compound whose main gate was guarded by a sentry and whose perimeter fence was crowned with concertina barbed wire. Once inside and past the sentry, who had been told of our imminent arrival, we were met by a lieutenant who thanked my driver and sent him on his way before taking me on a tour of the camp. The somewhat heart-shaped compound, covering about half a city block, contained an assortment of one- and two-story buildings. Some of these were left over from the decades of Japanese occupation

Author in front of leaflet bombs, Seoul City Air Base, Korea, 1953 (photographer
unidentified)

and now housed the company headquarters, a barracks, BOQ, general mess,
officers mess, machine shop, print shop, bomb and shell assembly shops, and
interestingly in view of our being on the outskirts of Seoul, a tower built of
railroad ties armed on its top with a swivel-mounted fifty-caliber machine gun.
As part of this defense armor there were a total of eighty unlined holes in the
ground, scattered around among the buildings, each of which was big enough
for two soldiers.

At this stage in the war, I was told that because of its purpose this particular compound qualified in theory at least as a primary target for the little
low-flying Bedcheck Charlies described in chapter 4. With a good gunner—the
camp had two of them—the swivel-mounted heavy machine gun was ideal
for shooting down these low, slow little planes. And the "foxholes," as they
were called by members of the company, would have been handy for watching the action. Alas, to the disappointment of the gunners, such action never
occurred.

The company, commanded by a lieutenant colonel whose staff was composed of four captains, six lieutenants, and ten sergeants, contained a com-
plement of nearly 120 Eighth Army personnel plus 25 South Korean civilian
guards and 10 South Korean civilians who helped with the cooking. As it was
explained to me, their single mission was that of printing propaganda leaflets—the loudspeaker soldiers were down the road in another compound—
and as such they were the only UN leaflet-producing operation in Korea. The

Leaflets packed in rolls for bomb delivery, Seoul, 1953 (courtesy of Paul A. Wolfgeher)

presses were Harris roll-type printers that turned out 24,000 5½ x
8½–inch leaflets an hour, which
with the help of South Korean civilian employees were loaded into
105mm or 155mm howitzer shells
or aerial bombs. Once the leaflets
were loaded they were trucked off
base through the "motor pool gate,"
which was the only other gate in the
compound's perimeter. The bombs
went to K-14 at Kimpo, and the shells,
by much longer routes, were shipped to various points along the Main Line of
Resistance (Paul A. Wolfgeher, personal communication).

Before taking leave from my newfound friends and teachers at the printing and assembling compound, I finished my leaflet assignment in what I have
since called "Leaflet School Advance" at Eighth Army Advance headquarters
on the other side of Seoul and across the street from my billet at Fifth Air
Force. There I was introduced to a cadre of about a dozen imaginative writers
and illustrators whose offices were in a small building near the one in which,
as described in chapter 4, I had listened to the spellbinding captain give his
morning position reports.

These writers and illustrators who composed the leaflets that were then
printed in the First L and L Company compound ranged in rank from major to
corporal. The writers were junior and field-grade officers and sergeants, most
of whom had college degrees and all of whom were experienced in this trade,
most of them having learned their skills as civilians working for newspapers
and magazines. The illustrators, typically noncoms, had similar professional
backgrounds.

Maintaining military discipline was hardly a priority. Once or twice a week
this congenial crew would get their heads together for the purpose of devel-
oping propaganda to put on paper. Their ideas derived first from general
knowledge, their keeping abreast of the progress of the war and its see-sawing

Korean civilians adding detonators to leaflet bombs at K-16, June 1953 (photo by author)

back and forth across Korea. One example of this general knowledge included an awareness of the social and economic changes that had resulted from the Chinese military occupancy of North Korea in 1950.

Further, the composers got their ideas from a variety of intelligence sources whose data were continuously relayed to the writing and illustrating cadre. These included, of course, the testimonies of newly captured or voluntarily surrendered enemy prisoners whose experiences would result in the sort of leaflet shown in plate 3. Others of the wizards' texts and drawings derived directly from requests of UN combat commanders who, as I have noted in reference to Eighth Army Japanese-based leaflet writers, often wanted leaflets designed to exploit particular situations on the battlefield.

The cadre's writers and illustrators were as helpful in teaching me what they were doing as were the soldiers I had met at the L and L Company compound. The writers, although in military uniforms, reminded me of the sophisticated and much-involved *Seattle Times* reporters I had met when I was a University of Washington undergraduate. And to my eye, the pictures being drawn by the illustrators were as good, if contextually different, as those of Bill Mauldin, the celebrated Second World War cartoonist.

As part of what I was learning from these impressive experts, I was given brief lessons in analyzing the contents and intended purposes of copies of both UN (Eighth Army) and enemy leaflets. I was also given a collection of one hundred different U.S. examples together with thirty-two CCF and NKPA printed messages to take home with me. Copies of all of the Eighth Army examples had been dropped or fired in recent combat, while those from the CCF and NKPA had been picked up on the battlefield by Eighth Army or other UN soldiers. Each of the collection's American leaflets was accompanied by a mimeographed sheet detailing its place and date of origin and other appropriate data, although the enemy leaflets quite naturally lacked accompanying explanations. What I learned at Eighth Army Advance, combined with library and archival data and personal interviews, provides for an appraisal of the leaflet campaign.

As I have remarked, in the Korean War leaflets were the primary UN psywar medium. They embraced several types of propaganda and were aimed at several audiences, but together their central shared purpose was that of reducing or impairing enemy morale for the purpose of persuading the enemy to quit fighting, not as an alternative but as an adjunct to winning the war by armed combat.

One first impression is that the leaflet endeavors of the United Nations and its Korean War enemies were noticeably congruent. According to former sergeant Paul A. Wolfgeher (personal communication), the propaganda objectives of the First Leaflet and Loudspeaker Company on the outskirts of Seoul were "adamantly" white hat, an attitude shared by the Company's Eighth Army conferees in Japan, and apparently by the CCF and NKPA people as well. In the U.S. Eighth Army, the first requirement in leaflet production was to tell the truth, or at least the truth as the army saw it. From what may be gleaned from our collection of CCF and NKPA printed messages, the enemy propaganda, generally speaking, also appears to have derived from the same perspective.

On both sides, the principal targets were "common" soldiers: neither commissioned officers nor ranking noncoms, such as sergeants, but rather those who in the U.S. Army would hold the rank of private. Privates or their equivalents were, with uncommon exceptions, both the youngest and the least educated soldiers in the war. On the enemy front, large numbers of CCF and NKPA troops were illiterate. Additionally, on both sides very large numbers of the lowermost ranking soldiers had been drafted as civilians into military service. These characteristics made them the most likely target for propaganda of this sort, being, as they were, especially susceptible to messages having to do with homesickness as well as messages relating to the more obvious physical discomforts and fear of getting killed that are common to life on a battlefield.

Among other examples, UN and Communist forces leaflets aimed at these common soldiers are illustrated in plates 3, 4, 5, 19, 20, and 23. As a rule of thumb, the "standard" UN leaflet measured about 5½ x 8½ inches, a size that allowed for its being hidden, read later in private, and passed on to other soldiers. Eighth Army composers and printers chose leaflet colors according to what they learned from intelligence sources regarding presumably "favorite" colors among enemy troops. Another factor in color choice was the natural hue of the terrain on which particular leaflets were to be dropped or fired. The leaflets needed to contrast enough with the landscape to make them easily seen.

A necessary adjunct to these messages—which as the viewer will note had their close parallels in those of the enemy—were safe conduct passes, which counting UN, Chinese, and North Korean productions were the most abundant leaflet type of the war. In size and content, UN, CCF, and NKPA leaflets are remarkably similar in their promises of good treatment to defecting soldiers (plates 1, 2, and 17).

Few data are available on the "evolution" during the war of safe conduct passes produced by the CCF and NKPA. As simple and straightforward as these passes (commonly called "surrender leaflets") appear, complications attending their effective distribution in combat resulted in the U.S. Eighth Army's printing six different styles or modifications of safe conduct passes by the war's end.

During the early stages of the conflict, U.S. safe conduct passes were widely distributed along the Main Line of Resistance and were continuously evaluated and updated, largely based on the accounts of our Chinese and North Korean prisoners of war. After 1952 when the fighting devolved to a stalemate, more planning was demanded in ways of delivering that would better allow enemy soldiers to recover the leaflets in this new era of limited patrolling and skirmishing.

Early in the war a total of one thousand North Korean prisoners had told UN interrogators that their greatest fear in using our safe conduct passes was that of getting killed in the attempt by UN troops or by their own officers. Increasingly as time passed, punishments were meted out by political officers to CCF and NKPA soldiers caught picking up or carrying surrender passes or any other UN leaflets. For example, Chinese political officers told the CCF soldiers that in addition to facing such dire punishments as execution if they attempted to surrender, their families at home would be made to suffer.

For good measure, Chinese troops were warned by their officers that UN leaflets, including the very large numbers made to resemble paper money, were contaminated with plague. Because of the threatened reprisals to soldiers' families, U.S. Eighth Army printers blotted from new runs the faces of smiling Chinese POWs that had appeared on earlier versions. Chinese Army political officers then told their troops that the faces had been covered to hide the signs of UN torture that had removed the prisoners' eyes. So the game went on and on, while for both sides the "common soldier" remained overwhelmingly the principal target.

One is impressed with the qualities of printing and composition expressed in nearly all Communist forces messages, about whose origins we know very little. All leaflets from both the CCF and NKPA were most likely produced in China. Based on his postwar inquiries, Paul A. Wolfgeher (personal communication), the former First L and L sergeant and printer, believes the enemy leaflets were made on small, freestanding presses, about two feet wide and three feet tall. These presses produced small leaflets (none larger than 8½ x 11 inches) in very large quantities. Wolfgeher thinks that batteries of these machines in Chinese cities not far north of the North Korean border printed leaflets of several themes for both countries simultaneously.

More intriguing, and more to the point of this book, is the question of who wrote the CCF and NKPA messages. Obviously they were well-educated men or women (see plates 17–33), having excellent command of the American idiom and in possession of then current American newspapers and magazines. Further, they were good to very good writers. But who were they? Guesses include that they were American missionaries or missionaries' children who had opted out of Christianity in favor of communism, that they were American military men who had voluntarily defected, that they were American prisoners who had been persuaded to write for the Communists, or, in Wolfgeher's opinion, that they were most likely native Chinese fellow travelers who had been longtime residents of the United States and who now had returned home. Still, the identities of these talented enemy writers remains a mystery.

In addition to the abundant "surrender" leaflets and those playing on homesickness and similar emotions of the kind mentioned above, other messages from both sides of the bloodless war were those that sought to cause dissension and distrust within enemy forces. Among other examples from the CCF and NKPA, the leaflet shown in plate 24 is intended to exploit the attitude among American GIs that the military brass was not playing fair in its rotation system; plate 28 reminds American black soldiers of their people's continuing mistreatment in the United States; plates 26 and 30 show images conveying that our American soldiers are actually fighting for the luxurious way of life of the American wealthy class. From the UN side, the leaflet shown in plate 7 tells NKPA soldiers that the Chinese give inferior equipment to North Korea, keeping the best weapons for themselves.

The U.S. Eighth Army psywar practitioners had an advantage over their enemy in that through most of the war the Chinese occupied North Korea. This condition permitted the UN to aim dozens of messages to both North Korean civilians and military personnel for the purpose of turning both of these audiences against the occupying CCF. The range of themes among this variety of leaflet, all of which express a single purpose, is illustrated among others by plate 13.

The Communist side, however, had an advantage in the fact that on balance U.S. troops were far better educated than those of the CCF and NKPA, thereby allowing for messages aimed at more sophisticated, perhaps more thoughtful soldiers who had knowledge and interest in the broader characteristics of the war. The lengthy leaflet shown in plate 32 is one such message, as are those shown in plates 30, 31, and 33. The U.S. Eighth Army replied in part to these and others like them with leaflets extolling the strengths and cohesiveness of the United Nations, as illustrated in plates 6 and 10.

Most unusual of all leaflets fired or dropped in the Korean War were those produced by Operation Moolah. The USAF was desperately anxious to get its hands on an intact, flyable MIG-15, the formidable Russian-built jet fighter of the kind that had shot down *Stardust 40*. It was well known that both Chinese and North Korean pilots were flying MIG-15s against UN targets, and it was widely believed that some of the MIGs were being flown by Soviet pilots as well.

Thus was created Operation Moolah in which otherwise identical leaflets printed in separate runs in three languages offered the first Chinese, North Korean, or Russian pilot who flew his MIG to one of our South Korean bases a reward of $100,000, a handsome sum for its time that in 2009 would be worth US$750,000. Further, the leaflets promised that any such pilot would receive political asylum in the Free World where his name would be kept "secret forever." MIG pilots who surrendered subsequent to the first defector were promised the same asylum but a smaller cash award of US$50,000. Accordingly, on April 26, 1953, more than one million leaflets were dropped along the Yalu River and another half-million were dropped near Sinuiju and Uiju airfields (see map) near the Chinese border.

These drops had the effect of radically reducing the number of MIGs over northernmost Korea for days afterward. But nothing was heard from the Communist air forces until on the September 21, 1953, fifty-six days after the signing of the Korea peace accords on July 27, the men in the control tower at K-14 at Kimpo on the edge of Seoul looked up to see a MIG-15, flaps and wheels down, coming in for a landing. The North Korean pilot, who had not seen or heard of the Moolah leaflets, had decided on his own hook to come over to the UN side. He was still given his cash reward and asylum (plate 16).

In evaluating the quality of our collection of Chinese and North Korean leaflets as compared with our U.S. Eighth Army examples, the unprejudiced observer must conclude that the enemy's were as good if not slightly better than those produced by the United States. One is impressed with what would seem to be the effectiveness of the enemy messages directed both at U.S. "private" soldiers and at those troops of better education and more sophisticated minds. However, in this regard it is interesting that combat soldiers, including mainly Americans, appear to have treated enemy leaflets picked up on the battlefield more as souvenirs to be sent to the folks back home than as anything in the way of persuasive documents. In researching this book, practically no evidence was found that Chinese and NKPA leaflet endeavors resulted in UN defections.

By comparison, then, how effective was the U.S. leaflet campaign? Here, the evidence squarely shows that it was notably successful. Decoded after the Korean War, Chinese authorities wrote that UN propaganda—more specifically U.S. propaganda—had made political control of the "Chinese Peoples Volunteer Army" difficult, and made the maintenance of morale among their ranks a serious challenge (Sandler 1999). Haas (2000) remarks that early in the war, among 120,000 UN prisoners, 12,000 ("plus or minus 6,000") were persuaded to surrender by U.S. psychological warfare, primarily leaflet, operations. He adds that the financial cost to the United States of "psywar capture" to conventional capture or kill was probably a ratio of 70 to 1 in favor of psychological warfare. Thus, while to both the Communist forces and those of the United Nations the Korean War was an unhappy draw, UN forces decisively won the leaflet campaign.

In the last week of June we seven young psywarriors who, masquerading as army lieutenants had been scattered across Korea, returned one by one to Fifth Air Force Advance, where we were sent across the gravel road to Eighth Army. There, in a brief, casual ceremony, we were awarded ribbons and campaign stars, and presented with certificates by Colonel Donald F. Hall, Chief of Eighth Army Psywar, attesting that (in my case) "during the period 27 May to 23 June 1953 . . . 2/Lt. J. M. Campbell . . . participated in Psychological Warfare Operations in combat against the Chinese Communist Forces and the North Korean Army." And finally, back across the street at Fifth, we were ordered, verbally of course, by the genial Major Scott, to find our way home as best we could.

This finding our way as best we could was literally true. Among other instructions, our orders to Korea included that "upon the compl of TDY off

w/rtn to proper sta." [Clark AFB]. Each of the seven of us carried several copies of the orders with which Major Scott advised us to first hitch a ride from
K-16 to Tachikawa and from there hitch another ride to Clark. The above-noted
inclusion, however, said nothing about how long we must take in returning
to proper station, and for Bill Samuels (see acknowledgments) and me it took
more than a memorable month.

Notes

Introduction

1. In writing this introduction I have relied upon sources that, in my opinion, are important to an understanding of the history of the Korean War and more specifically to the nature of the U.S. psychological warfare efforts in that conflict. Some of these sources are cited individually in the following text; others include: Ambrose 1990; Ballingrud 2003; Breuer 1996; Goldstein and Maihafer 2000; Haas 2000; Hickey 2000; Sandler 1999; Sulzberg 1966; Thornton 2000. The textual citations appear in the bibliography in more detail.

2. While attending the Potsdam Conference in the last half of July 1945, President Truman told Russia's premier, Joseph Stalin, that the United States had just successfully detonated an atom bomb that could hasten the end of the war in Japan. Truman's intent was to get Stalin to authorize a Soviet front against Japan. The result was an increase in Soviet nuclear weapons development directed by Stalin on August 7, 1945.

3. The Cairo Conference—held in December 1943 among the leaders of Great Britain (Churchill), Nationalist China (Chiang Kai-shek), and the United States (Roosevelt)—produced the Cairo Declaration, which covered the return of conquered Japanese territory to nations from which they had been taken. Among these territories the island of Formosa (Taiwan) was promised to China and Korea was to become an independent nation. These articles of the Cairo Declaration were agreed to by Russia (Stalin) at the Potsdam Conference and during the peace talks at Yalta at the close of the war in Europe in 1945.

4. Soviet Ambassador Jacob Malik had been advised by UN Secretary-General Trygve Lie that it would be in the best interests of his country for him to attend the afternoon meeting but he had refused.

5. Stalin had allowed 1,500 MIG aircraft and Russian pilots to be positioned along the Chinese coast off Taiwan. The UN blockade of Korean waters following Kim Il-sung's advance on Seoul thwarted Mao's plan to attack Taiwan with the planes.

6. With Syngman Rhee's approval these ROK soldiers, named Korean Augmentation to U.S. Army (KATUSA), were housed, armed, and gladly accepted by American combat teams.

7. General Clark had replaced General Ridgway, who had moved to Europe to assume command of NATO forces from General Eisenhower in May 1952. General Maxwell Taylor replaced General Van Fleet as commander of the Eighth Army.

8. On June 25, 1952, U.S. Air Force and Navy fighter bombers destroyed the Sup'ung/Suiho hydroelectric generating plant (see map) on the Yalu River along the northwestern Korean border with Manchuria. Continuing sorties against North Korean hydroelectric complexes put the country in the dark for two weeks and impacted all Manchurian and Siberian manufacturing facilities. On August 25, 1952, a successful U.S. air attack of the Najin shipping center, railway terminals, bridges, and military supply depots, just nineteen miles south of the North Korean/Soviet border, disrupted the flow of arms to General Peng's armies. Bombing raids continued into 1953 as President Eisenhower sought to leverage Communist representatives at truce talks in Panmunjom.

Chapter One

1. Haas 1997 is the principle background source for this chapter. Other contributors are Brown 1982; Pennsylvania Biographies 2008; Johnson 1974; Herbert A. Mason Jr., e-mail message to Katherine Kallestad, October 10, 2008; and Air Resupply and Communications Association 2008, the latter of which is quoted in the text.

2. A squadron is an air force administrative unit within a wing; see further in this chapter.

3. Serving under an air force unit's commanding officer, an adjutant is its chief day-to-day administrator.

Chapter Two

1. For an instructive sampling of the range of psychological warfare operations practiced by the Allies in the European Theater, see: Delmer 1962; Hemingway 1986; Masterman 2000; Montagu 1953; Moss 2001; and Stevenson 2007.

2. For an account of other adventures and misadventures of the 580th, see Haas 1997, 111–24.

Chapter Three

1. See Krugler 2000; Nelson 1997; and Tyson 1983 for detailed histories of the Voice of America.

2. In 1952 and early 1953 the ARCS wings departed Mountain Home for good. In September 1952 the 580th was deployed to the U.S. Wheelus Field in Libya. The 582nd was deployed to Great Falls AFB, Montana, in May 1953. After the war, in February 1954—by then reduced to group, rather than wing status with a total of six hundred instead of twelve hundred officers and airmen—it was sent to Molesworth Royal Air Force Base in England.

3. Merchant marine officers hold equivalent reserve ranks in one of the other branches of service, usually the navy. In all probability, the skipper of the USNS *David C. Shanks*, a lieutenant commander, was a reserve U.S. Navy lieutenant commander.

4. In covert operations, circumstances sometimes required an individual of one rank to temporarily assume another, usually higher, rank.

5. I was given most of both types later in the year after I had been promoted to first lieutenant.

6. The following examples of black operations in Korea are based on Burns 1998; Haas 1997 and 2000; Logan 2007; Sullivan 2007; and personal communications in 2008 with retired air force officers Colonel Michael E. Haas, Lieutenant Colonel William M. Samuels, Major Robert F. Sullivan, and retired Master Sergeant Yancy D. Mailes.

7. One of the "dogs" and "cats" moved quietly in Korea was president-elect Dwight D. Eisenhower, who was not only fulfilling his promise to voters by going to Korea to begin the end of an unpopular war, but who also wanted to see his son, Major John Eisenhower. One of the 581st ARSq [H] crews handled the classified transportation for Eisenhower's December 1952 visit.

Chapter Four

1. With the surrender of the Japanese at the end of the Second World War, Korea was restored to its ancient national status after having endured thirty-five years of military and civil occupation as Japan's Chosen Province. Numerous schools, businesses, and landmarks still had Japanese names and many maps in use by UN Command had been taken from the Japanese military.

2. On May 31, 1953, in a routine change of command Lieutenant General Samuel E. Anderson replaced Lieutenant General Glenn Barcus.

3. The designation "one five five howitzer" refers to a cannon whose bore diameter is 155mm, or about 6 inches. Howitzers loft their shells in arcs. Typically, the men who load and fire them never see their targets, whose distant positions are plotted by forward observers who relay the proper coordinates to the gun crews. This howitzer had a maximum effective range of about eight miles. The NKPA counterpart, made in the USSR, had a bore diameter of 122mm (5 inches). Both sides fought the war with other large-caliber guns of various sizes. An impressively large weapon, but of limited deployment in Korea, was the U.S. 203mm (8-inch) howitzer mounted on the

chassis of a Sherman tank. With this exception, however, no field guns in the war were larger than our "one five five."

4. The Scottish officer's remark, meant here as a friendly gibe, referred to the infamous "Battle of Glencoe," in which Campbells loyal to English King William III slaughtered dozens of innocent members of Clan MacDonald, a deed that while it happened in AD 1692 is remembered still in Scotland.

5. My promotion to first lieutenant had nothing to do with my being in Korea. After three years of good behavior, newly commissioned second lieutenants were promoted automatically. My promotion orders had been forwarded to me from Thirteenth Air Force at Clark.

6. Mortars, like howitzers, but usually smaller, short-barreled, and manned by two or three gunners, loft their shells in arcs.

Chapter Five

1. Chief literary sources for this chapter include Breuer 1996; Haas 2000; Hickey 1999; Jones 1997; Sandler 1999; and Wolfgeher 2008.

2. Abbreviations used in plate description headings are as follows:

APO 301=Army Post Office in Korea
APO 500=Army Post Office in Japan
AU=Army Unit
EUSAK=Eighth United States Army in Korea.

Bibliography

Air Resupply and Communications Association. 2008. "Mountain Home Air Force Base." http://www.arcassn.org (accessed November 4).

Ambrose, Stephen E. 1990. *Eisenhower: Soldier and President.* New York: Simon and Schuster.

Appleman, Roy E. 1989. *Disaster in Korea: The Chinese Confront MacArthur.* College Station: Texas A&M University Press.

Arlington National Cemetery. 2008. "Colonel John Riley 'Killer' Kane, USAF." www.arlingtoncemetery.net/jrkane.htm (accessed October 10).

Ballingrud, David. 2003. "Korea: The Forgotten War, June 25, 1950–July 27, 1953." *St. Petersburg Times* (commemorative series), 13A–15A.

Bank, Aaron. 1986. *From OSS to Green Berets: The Birth of Special Forces.* Novato, CA: Presidio Press.

Bennett, Kitty, and Steve Madden. 2003. "Korean War." *St. Petersburg Times,* July 20, 15A, map and statistics.

Blair, Clay. 1987. *The Forgotten War: America in Korea, 1950–1953.* New York: Times Books.

Brady, James. 2003. "A Sacred Place Where We Fought." *Parade Magazine,* May 23, 4–6.

Breuer, William B. 1996. *Shadow Warriors: The Covert War in Korea.* New York: John Wiley and Sons.

Brown, Anthony C. 1982. *Wild Bill Donovan: The Last Hero.* New York: Times Books.

Bruning, John R. Jr. 2000. *Crimson Sky: The Air Battle for Korea.* Dulles, VA: Brassey's.

Burns, Robert. 1998. "China Honors Two Spies Who Survived Imprisonment in China for 20 Years." *St. Joseph (MO) New Press for Associated Press,* July 4.

Campbell, John Martin. 1997. *Few and Far Between: Moments in the North American Desert.* Santa Fe: Museum of New Mexico Press.

Catchpole, Brian. 2001. *The Korean War.* London: Constable and Robinson.

Clark, Mark Wayne. 1954. *From the Danube to the Yalu.* 1st ed. New York: Harper Collins.

Deerfield, Eddie. 2002. "Korea's Bloodless Battle: A Story of Psychological Warfare." *Graybeards* 16, no. 4:12, 14. Buford, SC: Finisterre Publishing.

Delmer, Sefton. 1962. *Black Boomerang: An Autobiography.* London: Martin Secker and Warburg.

Easton, Stewart C. 1968. *The World Since 1945.* San Francisco: Chandler Publishing Company.

Franklin, Warren. 1953. *Pacific Stars and Stripes,* June 18.

Futrell, Robert F. 1983. *The United States Air Force in Korea, 1950–1953.* Washington, DC: Office of Air Force History, U.S. Air Force.

Georgetown University. 1952. *The Institute of Languages and Linguistics, School of Foreign Service, Program of Instruction 1951–1953.* Washington, DC: Georgetown University.

———. 2002a. *The Institute of Languages and Linguistics, Faculty 1952–53.* Washington, DC: Lauinger Library, Special Collections Division.

———. 2002b. *Georgetown University History—World War II.* http://data.georgetown.edu/slides, pg. 14 (accessed May 6).

Goldstein, Donald M., and Harry J. Maihafer. 2000. *The Korean War: The Story and Photographs.* Washington, DC: Brassey's.

Goulden, Joseph. 1982. *Korea, The Untold Story of the War.* New York: Times Books.

Gugeler, Russell A. 1954. *Combat Actions in Korea.* Rev. ed. 1970. Washington, DC: Combat Forces Press.

Haas, Michael E. 1997. *Apollo's Warriors: U.S. Air Force Special Operations During the Cold War.* Maxwell Air Force Base, AL: Air University Press.

———. 2000. *In the Devil's Shadow: UN Special Operations During the Korean War.* Annapolis, MD: Naval Institute Press.

Halberstam, David. 2007. *The Coldest Winter: America and the Korean War.* New York: Hyperian.

Hallion, Richard P. 1986. *The Naval Air War in Korea.* Baltimore: Nautical and Aviation Publishing Company of America.

Hammel, Eric M. 1981. *Chosin: Heroic Ordeal of the Korean War.* New York: Vanguard Press.

Hastings, Max. 1987. *The Korean War.* London: Book Club Associates.

Heinlein, Robert A. 1951. *The Puppet Masters.* 1st ed. New York: Doubleday and Co.

Hemingway, Jack. 1986. *Misadventures of a Fly Fisherman.* Toronto: Key Porter Books.

Hickey, Michael. 2000. *The Korean War: The West Confronts Communism, 1950–1953.* London: John Murray.

Huston, James Alvin. 1989. *Guns and Butter, Powder and Rice: U.S. Army Logistics in the Korean War.* Selinsgrove, PA: Susquehanna University Press.

Johnson, Arthur M. N.d. "The Origin and Development of the United States Air Force Psychological Warfare Program, 1946–1952." Prepared for the USAF Historical Division, declassified October 18, 1974.

Jones, Robert W. Jr. 2007. "The Ganders: Strategic Psywar in the Far East. Part 1: Introduction and Movement to the Far East"; Part 2: "The Ganders: 1st Radio Broadcasting and Leaflet Group Conducts Psywar in Korea." *Veritas—Journal of Army Special Operations History* 2, no. 3:59–65; 3, no. 3:41–58.

Kaufman, Burton I. 1986. *The Korean War: Challenges in Crisis, Credibility and Command.* Philadelphia: Temple University Press.

————. 1999. The Korean Conflict. Westport, CT: Greenwood Press.

Kelly, Orr. 1996. *From a Dark Sky: U.S. Air Force Special Operation.* Novato, CA: Presidio Press.

Koch, R. W. 2007. "Death Valley Albatross." Air Resupply and Communications Association. www.arcassn.org/albatross.htm (accessed January 2).

Kohart, Georgia. 2001. *Defiance (Ohio) Crescent-News,* January 28.

Knox, Donald. 1985. *The Korean War, Pusan to Chosin: An Oral History.* 1st ed. New York: Harcourt Brace Jovanovich.

Krugler, David F. 2000. *The Voice of America and the Domestic Propaganda Battles, 1945–1953.* Columbia: University of Missouri Press.

Leviero, Anthony. N.d. *How We Are Fighting the Battle for Men's Minds.* New York: New York Times Washington Bureau.

Logan, Ray. 1997. "Our 'Lost' Detachment in Korea." *Arc Light,* January.

MacCloskey, Monro. 1969. *Alert the Fifth Force: Counterinsurgency, Unconventional Warfare, and Psychological Operations of the United States Air Force in Special Air Warfare.* New York: Richard Rosen Press.

MacDonald, R. Ross. 1967. "Leon Dostert." www.mt-archive.info/MacDonald -1967.

Maeder, Jay. 2000. "Better Dead than Red—Oksana Kasenkina, August 1948." *Big Town/Big Time Series.* www.nydailynews.com/archives/news/2000/ 10/2000.

Malcom, Ben S., with Ron Martz. 1996. *White Tigers: My Secret War in North Korea.* Dulles, VA: Brassey's.

Masterman, J. C. 2000. *The Double-cross System.* New York: Lyons Press.

Miller, David. 2000. *The Illustrated Directory of Tanks of the World from World War I to the Present Day.* Osceola, WI: MBI Publishing Company.

Miller, John Jr., et al. 1956. *Korea, 1951–1953.* Washington, DC: Defense Department, Army, Office of the Chief of Military History, U.S. Government Printing Office.

Montagu, Ewen. 1953. *The Man Who Never Was.* Philadelphia: J. B. Lippincott Company.

Morrissey, Jim. 1953. *Pacific Stars and Stripes,* June 18.

Moss, W. Stanley. 2001. *Ill Met by Moonlight.* London: The Folio Society.

Mossman, Billy C. 1990. *Ebb and Flow, November 1950–July 1951.* Washington, DC: Center of Military History.

NationMaster.com. 2009. "Edmund A. Walsh." http://www.nationmaster.com/ encyclopedia/Edmund-A.-Walsh (accessed February).

Naval Historical Center. 2009. "USNS *David C. Shanks* (T-AP-180), 1943–1973." http://www.history.navy.mil/photos/sh-usn/usnsh-d/ap180.htm (accessed February 12).

Nelson, Michael. 1997. *War of the Black Heavens: The Battles of Western Broadcasting in the Cold War*. Syracuse, NY: Syracuse University Press.

New York Times. 1991. "John Pauker, 70, Dies; Ex-U.S. Aide and Poet." January 25.

Paddock, Alfred H. Jr. 1982. *U.S. Army Special Warfare: Its Origins*. Washington, DC: National Defense University.

Pennsylvania Biographies. 2008. "Henry 'Hap' Arnold, Air Force Hero." www. geocities.com/heartland/43547/arnold.html (accessed July 24).

Pickering, John M. "The U.S. and the Land of Morning Calm." *PeaceReview*, Winter/Spring 1991, 38–42.

Rearden, Jim. 1990. *Cracking the Zero Mystery*. Harrisburg, PA: Stackpole Books.

Sandler, Stanley. 1999. *The Korean War: No Victors, No Vanquished*. Lexington: University Press of Kentucky.

Stevenson, William. 2007. *Spymistress, The Life of Vera Atkins, The Greatest Female Secret Agent of World War II*. 1st ed. New York: Arcade Publishing.

Sullivan, Robert F. 1995. "The 581st's Helicopters." *Arc Light,* January. Also see arcassn.org/581-helicopters.html (accessed January 2, 2007).

Sulzberger, C. L. 1966. *World War II*. New York: American Heritage/Bonanza Books.

Summers, Robert E., ed. 1972. *American Weapons of Psychological Warfare*. New York: Arno Press.

Time Books. 2002. "The Unexpected War." In *Time Goes to War*. New York: Time Books.

Thornton, Richard C. 2000. *Odd Man Out: Truman, Stalin, Mao and the Origins of the Korean War*. Washington, DC: Brassey's.

Toland, John. 1991. *In Mortal Combat: Korea, 1950–1953*. New York: William Morrow and Company.

Tyson, James L. 1983. *U.S. International Broadcasting and National Security*. New York: Ramapo Press.

VOA (Voice of America). 2003. *Post World War II Era. 1942–2002*. http://www. voa.gov (accessed January 17).

Whelan, Richard. 1990. *Drawing the Line: The Korean War 1950–1953*. 1st ed. London: Faber and Faber.

Wolfgeher, Paul A. 2008. Unpublished notes and manuscripts on the role of propaganda leaflets in Korean War. Independence, MO.

Yakima Daily Republic. 1950. June 26, 27, 28; September 15; November 27.

Zaloga, Steven J., and George Balin. 1994. *Tank Warfare in Korea 1950–1953*. New Territories, Hong Kong: Concord Publications Company.

Index

Page numbers in italic text indicate illustrations.

A-26 (Douglas A-26 Invader medium bomber), 99
Acheson, Dean (secretary of state), 6, 7, 11
adjutant, 38, 166*n*3
aircraft: A-26, 99; accidents of, 40–41; B-29s, 19, 21, 40, *41, 47,* 63–64, *64,* 73–75, 98–99; C-46s, 97, 99; C-47s, 14, 99; C-124s, 76; H-119A helicopters, 72–73, 167*n*7; MIG-15 jet fighters, 73, *128–29,* 162–63, 165*n*5; at Mountain Home Air Force Base, 40–42, *41, 42;* of NKPA, 85; Operation Moolah for, *128–29,* 162–63; SA-16s, 40–42, *42,* 70, *71;* for secrecy, 72–73
air force, 4; shortages in, 8, 14
Air Intelligence Service Squadron (AISS), 72
air resupply, 4
Air Resupply and Communications Service (ARCS), ix; activation of, 4, 15–16, 31; CIA and, 33, 74; deactivation of, 21; requirements of, 33; squadrons within, 42; volunteers in, 43; wings of, 33–34. *See also* 581st ARCS Wing

Air University (Montgomery, Alabama), 4
AISS. *See* Air Intelligence Service Squadron
Allen, Second Lieutenant Jack, 45, 46
Anderson, General Samuel E., 78, 167*n*2
APO. *See* Army Post Office
APO 301. *See* Army Post Office in Korea
APO 500. *See* Army Post Office in Japan
ARCS. *See* Air Resupply and Communications Service
army: KATUSA as, 13, 166*n*6; OJT with, 74–75. *See also specific armies, divisions*
Army Post Office (APO), 155
Army Post Office in Japan (APO 500), 168*n*2
Army Post Office in Korea (APO 301), 168*n*2
Army Unit (AU), 168*n*2
Arnold, Colonel John K., 33; shoot-down of, 19, 21, 63–64, *64,* 73–75
Arnold, General Henry ("Hap"), 31–32
atomic cannon, 93, *93*
attack(s), 13, 18; aftermaths of, 87, 92; by Bedcheck Charlies, 85–88; at broadcasting studio, 83; first, by North Korea, ix, 7–8, 24; at intelligence squad, 94–95; warnings of, *118–19*

Attaway, John, 46
AU. *See* Army Unit

B-29s, 19, 21, 40, *41, 47,* 63–64, *64,* 73–75; U.S./ UN leaflets from, 98–99
Barcus, Glenn, 167*n*2
Barrett, Edward W. (assistant secretary of state), 56–57
"Battle of Glencoe," 85, 168*n*4
BDA. *See* Northern Border Defense Army
Bedcheck Charlies, 85–88
Beeks, Colonel Herbert W., 34–35, 43
Beyer, H. Otley (anthropologist), 91–92
birding: at Central Pacific, 63; at Clark Field, 67–68; at Eye Corps, 88–89
black hats: Cochran as, 69; Hedrick as, 68–69; Korean women as, 71–72; missions of, 70–74; Nichols as, 7, 72; Sustrick as, 69; white hats v., 40, 43, 68, 73
Bradley, General Omar N., 8
Brian, Corporal, *81*
British, 92; NKPA/CCF leaflets to, *147–48;* reinforcements, 13; visit to, 83–85
British QF (Quick Firing) twenty-five pounder, 99–100
broadcasting studio, 82–83

173

Brody, Second Lieutenant
  Fred, 51

C-46s (Curtiss C-46
  Commando), 97, 99
C-47s, 14, 99
C-124s, 76
Cairo Declaration, 165n3
Campbell, Donald MacIver,
  92
Campbell, George, 35
Campbell, Jack, 81, 156
Campbell, Second Lieutenant
  J. M., 163
Campbell, Susan Lombard
  Horsley, 23, 26, 27,
  37–38, 58, 92
CCF. See Chinese Communist
  Forces
CCRAK, 72
Central Intelligence Agency
  (CIA), 3, 4, 33, 74
Chapman, First Lieutenant,
  45
Chicom (Chinese
  Communists), 93–96
China, 2–3, 12, 162; BDA of,
  10–11, 24; Taiwan v.,
  10, 165n3. See also Mao
  Tse-tung
China-Burma-India, 32
Chinese Communist Forces
  (CCF), 93–96, 155. See
  also leaflet(s) (NKPA/
  CCF)
Chou En-lai, 74
CIA. See Central Intelligence
  Agency
Clark, General Mark W., 20,
  128–29, 166n7
Clark Field (Clark Air Force
  Base): birding at, 67–68;
  "intelligence matters" at,
  69, 70, 167n5; Japanese
  occupation of, 65; leaf-
  lets at, 68; leaving, 76;
  Negritos at, 65–67, 66;
  setting of, 64–65; social
  assignments at, 69–70;
  TDY from, 75
Cochran, First Lieutenant
  Drexel ("Barney"), 69
Cold War, 3–6

Collins, Dr. Henry B., Jr., 53
communism. See China;
  Soviet Union
Corsair, 87

deaths: from disease, 17–18;
  from Korean War, 1,
  17, 20
Deerfield, Eddie, 97
Donovan, William J. ("Wild
  Bill"), 31, 32–33
Dostert, Colonel Leon E.,
  49–50, 53–54
Dulles, John Foster (secre-
  tary of state), 20, 34

Eareckson, Colonel William
  O., 33
Eastern Europe, 5
Eighth Army Far East
  Command (Tokyo), 98
Eighth Army First
  Loudspeaker and Leaflet
  Company: action in
  Korea begins, 15; intro-
  duction to, 155–56;
  presses at, 156–57
Eighth United States Army in
  Korea (EUSAK), 168n2.
  See also Eye Corps
Eisenhower, Dwight (presi-
  dent elect), 21, 49,
  166n7; Korean visit
  by, 167n7; POWs and,
  19–20; PW and, 31
Eisenhower, Major John, 19,
  167n7
Elizabeth (queen), 92
EUSAK. See Eighth United
  States Army in Korea
Eye Corps (Eighth Army's
  First Corps): air raid
  shelter of, 87–88; alco-
  hol at, 88; Bedcheck
  Charlies and, 85–88;
  birding at, 88–89; British
  battalion and, 83–84;
  broadcasting studio
  of, 82–83; intelligence
  squad and, 93–95; interrogation in, 95–96; MLR
  and, 79–81; MSR and,
  80; orders at, 80;

password and, 84; rank
  in, 90, 168n5; signs near,
  83–84, 84, 94

Far East Command's "Liaison
  Group" (FEC/LG), 13
FEC/LG. See Far East
  Command's "Liaison
  Group"
Fifth Air Force Advance, 77,
  163; Bedcheck Charlies
  at, 85–86; briefings at,
  78–79
Finch, Second Lieutenant, 45
First Loudspeaker and
  Leaflet Company ("L and
  L Company"), 98
First World War, 97
Fish, Colonel Robert W., 34
580th ARCS Wing, 33, 34
581st ARCS Wing, 33;
  assignment to, 30–31;
  deployment of, 18–19,
  61; duties of, 34, 72;
  helicopter squadron
  of, 72–73, 167n7; jokes
  for, 45–47; leaks from,
  73–74; rank in, 69,
  167n4; roll call for, 46;
  scarcities in, 43–44;
  secrecy of, 16–17, 31,
  39, 54, 69–70; TDY and,
  47–48; training in, 16,
  18–19, 43–47
581st Reproduction
  Squadron, 33
582nd ARCS Wing, 33, 34
flak vests, 81, 81
Fleet, General Van, 166n7
Fort Riley, Kansas, 2, 14, 16
Franklin, Warren (civilian
  writer), 86–87
funding: NSC and, 5–6; for
  VOA, 56–57

G3 operations, 80–85. See
  also Eye Corps
Gallagher, Master Sergeant,
  63
Georgetown University,
  43; administrators at,
  49–50; classroom at,
  49–50; courses at, 50–52;

coursework at, 53; duties after, 55; faculty at, 50–52; graduation from, 53–54; orders to, 48; Pentagon and, 51–52; secrecy at, 54; students at, 51

germ warfare, 18, 19

Gilbert, Colonel Lawrence C., 64

Greene, Colonel J. Woodall, 8–9

Grill, Second Lieutenant Charlie, 51, 74

Gsovski, Vladimir, 50–51

Gunther, Erna (professor), 26

H-119A helicopters, 72, 73, 167n7

Haas, Colonel Michael, ix, 40, 64

Hall, Colonel Donald F., 78, 163

Han River, 77, 88–89

Harrison, William, 153–54

Hedrick, Lieutenant Colonel, 68–69

helicopters (H-119A), 72; "dogs and cats" from, 73, 167n7

Hepzibah, Mam'selle, 61

Hill, W. W. ("Nibs") (professor), 26

Hillis, Second Lieutenant Angelo, 30

housing: at Mountain Home Air Force Base, 37, 37; secrecy and, 39

howitzers, 83, 167n3; mortars v., 168n6; U.S./UN leaflets from, 99–100, 155–56

HRRI. See Human Resource Research Institute

Human Resource Research Institute (HRRI), 32

IBS. See International Broadcasting System

Identify Friend or Foe (IFF), 76–77

IFF. See Identify Friend or Foe

intelligence operatives. See black hats

International Broadcasting System (IBS), 55

interrogation: cigarettes in, 96; illiteracy in, 96; on PW, 96; treatment and, 95–96

Japan, 2, 98, 168n2

Japanese-Americans, 25–26

Japanese occupation, 65, 77, 167n1; Negritos and, 67

Johnson, Louis (secretary of defense), 7

K-16, 72

Kai-shek, Generalissimo Chiang, 5, 11–12, 138, 165n3

Kallestad, Katherine, 1–21

Kane, Colonel John R. ("Killer"), 33–35

Kasenkina, Oksana, 60

KATUSA. See Korean Augmentation to the U.S. Army

Khadduri, Majid, 50

Kim (ROK soldier), 81, 81–83

Kim Il-sung (premier): in NKPA/CCF leaflets, 130; propaganda from, 9–10; Stalin and, 3, 5; in U.S./UN leaflets, 120

KMAG. See Korean Military Advisory Group

Kohler, Foy (VOA chief), 56, 58

Korea: arriving in, 76–77; division of, 2, 5; Japanese occupation of, 67, 77, 167n1. See also North Korea; South Korea

Korean Augmentation to the U.S. Army (KATUSA), 13, 166n6

Korean Military Advisory Group (KMAG), 5

"L and L Company," 98

leaflet(s) (NKPA/CCF): to black soldiers, 145–46; to British soldiers, 147–48; Christmas in, 135–36, 138–39, 144; on class, 144, 149, 150; for dissension, 135–38, 141, 144–50, 161; education and, 149–54, 162; effectiveness of, 163; on hiding, 142–43; Kim Il-sung in, 130; on POWs, 131, 153; quality of, 161, 163; on rotation, 132, 134, 141; safe conduct passes as, 130, 160; targets of, 159–60; U.S./UN leaflets v., 159–63; against war, 133, 135–38, 151–54; writers of, 161

leaflet(s) (U.S./UN), ix–x; from airdrop packages, 100; in artillery shells, 98–100, 99, 100; attack warnings in, 118–19; in bombs, 156–57, 156–58; Chinese occupation and, 162; for dissension, 111–13, 120–25; on education, 120–21; effectiveness of, 163; from field guns, 111, 155; on food, 122–23; by foot, 155; on home v. war, 106; from howitzers, 99–100, 155–56; ideas for, 157–58; Kim Il-sung in, 120; Mao Tsetung in, 111–14; NKPA/CCF leaflets v., 159–63; on NKPA's inferiority, 111–13; from North Korea, 101–2; numbers of, 97–98; on Operation Moolah, 162–63; physical characteristics of, 159–60; POWs and, 20; printing of, 98, 156–57; purposes of, 159; quality of, 163; on rainstorm escapes, 104–5; requests for, 98; for ROK, 97–98; safe conduct passes as, 101–3, 107–8, 160–61; Stalin in, 112–14; targets for, 159–60; on trails,

155; on UN, *109–10, 116–17,* 162; on women's suffering, *124–27*
"Leaflet School Advance": lessons at, 158–59; personnel at, 156
Lie, Trygve, 165*n4*
Lincoln, Abraham (president), 96

MacArthur, General Douglas, 7, 49, 67, 97–98; amphibious attack by, 13, 18; for bombing, 9; Chiang Kai-shek and, 11; removal of, 18; retreat and, 15; South Korea and, 5; Truman v., 11, 18; as U.N. Supreme Commander, 10
MacCloskey, Colonel Monro, 4
Macrides, Second Lieutenant Nicholas, 30, 36
Main Line of Resistance (MLR) ("the Line"): blackouts and, 80; bunkers and, 82–83; Eye Corps and, 79–81; G3 operations and, 80–85; Ross and, 92–95
Main Supply Route (MSR), 79, 79–80, 84
Malik, Jacob (ambassador), 11, 12, 18, 165*n4*
Manhattan: restaurants in, 60–61. *See also* Voice of America
Mao Tse-tung (chairman), 3, 96; BDA and, 10–11; Chiang Kai-shek v., 5; North Korea and, 12, 14; Stalin and, 5, 10–11, 165*n5*; truce for, 21; on U.S./UN leaflets, *111–14*
Marshall, George C. (secretary of state), 3–4
MATS. *See* Military Air Transport Service
Maudlin, Bill, 158
Maxwell Air Force Base (Montgomery, Alabama), 4

McClure, Brigadier General Robert A., 98
McConnell, Joe (fighter pilot), 73
merchant marines, 62; officers of, 167*n3*
MIG-15 jet fighters, 73, *128–29,* 162–63, 165*n5*
Military Air Transport Service (MATS), 6, 31
Military Payment Certificates (MPCs), 91
MLR. *See* Main Line of Resistance
Morrisey, Corporal Jim, 86
mortars, 94, 168*n6*
Mountain Home Air Force Base, 31–35, *35, 36;* adjustment to, 27–28; aircraft at, 40–42, *41, 42;* assignments at, 38; command in, 29–30; discrimination and, 30; housing at, 37, *37;* nature on, 28–29; orders to, 27; return to, 61; soldiers' backgrounds at, 37–38, 44; testing on, 29
MPCs. *See* Military Payment Certificates
MSR. *See* Main Supply Route
Muccio, John (ambassador), 5, 12
Murdock, George Peter (professor), 70

Nam Il, General, *152–53*
National Security Council (NSC): funding and, 5–6; for military buildup, 5; secrecy from, 4; Soviet's information from, 6; on VOA, 3
NATO. *See* North Atlantic Treaty Organization
navy: enlistment in, 23; merchant marines v., 62, 167*n3*
Negritos, 65; hunts of, 66, *66;* Japanese occupation and, 67; MacArthur and, 67; research with, 66–67
New York Times, 7

Nichols, Master Sergeant Donald, 7, 72
NKPA. *See* North Korean Peoples' Army
North Atlantic Treaty Organization (NATO), 59
Northern Border Defense Army (BDA), 10–11, 24
North Korea: bombing of, 20, 166*n8;* first attack by, ix, 7–8, 24; leaflet from, *101–2;* Mao Tse-tung and, 12, 14; map of, *xiv;* Pusan in, 10–12
North Korean Peoples' Army (NKPA): advance of, 12; aircraft from, 85; howitzers of, 167*n3;* Kim and, 82–83; MLR and, 81; propaganda from, 10; Stalin for, 5
NSC. *See* National Security Council

Office of Strategic Services (OSS), 2; for CIA, 33; Donovan for, 32–33
Office of War Information (OWI), 2
Oletta, Sergeant, 80, *81;* adventures with, 81–85; broadcasting studio with, 82–83
on-the-job training (OJT), 55; with army, 74–75
Operation Moolah, *128–29,* 162–63
Osborn, Douglas, 24
OSS. *See* Office of Strategic Services
OTJ. *See* on-the-job training
OWI. *See* Office of War Information

Pacific Stars and Stripes, 86–87
Panikkar, K. M. (ambassador), 12
Partridge, General Earle E., 72
Patton, General George S., 12
Pauker, John (policy guidance officer), 58–60

peace talks, 18, *152–54*; POWs and, 20
Peng, General Teh-huai, 20
Pentagon, 51–52
Pershing tank, 94
Philippines: Beyer in, 91–92; *Stardust 40* news in, 19, 21, 63–64, *64*, 73–74. *See also* Clark Field
Potsdam Conference, 165*nn*2–3
POWs. *See* prisoners of war
prisoners of war (POWs), 19; exchange of, 20; interrogation of, 96; leaflets and, 20, *131*, *153*
propaganda, 3–4; data for, 44; from Kim Il-sung, 9–10; from NKPA, 10
psychological warfare (PW): courses on, 52–53; First World War and, 97; Korean partisans and, 71–72; McClure and, 98; purpose of, 4; range of, 39–40; secrecy in, 39; white-hat v. black-hat, 40, 43, 68, 73; in World War II, 31, 32, 97
The Psychological Warfare and Intelligence School, 43
Psychological Warfare Branch (PWB), Far East Command, 8–9
Psychological Warfare Division, U.S. Air Force, 6, 14, 31
psywar. *See* psychological warfare (PW)
Pusan, North Korea, 10–12
PW. *See* psychological warfare
PWB. *See* Psychological Warfare Branch

QF. *See* British QF (Quick Firing) twenty-five pounder
Queen's Palace, 88, 89
Quirino, Elpidio (president), 70

Radio Moscow, 54
RAND Corporation, 4, 32
rank, 167*n*3; adjutant, 38, 166*n*3; in Eye Corps, 90, 168*n*5; in 581st ARCS Wing, 69, 167*n*4
reinforcements: from Britain/Australia, 13; from South Korea, 13, 166*n*6
Reiter, Paul (professor), 27
Republic of Korea (ROK): intelligence squad of, 93–95; KMAG for, 5; leaflets for, 97–98. *See also* Kim
Reserve Officers Training Corps (ROTC), 23; for air force, 24
Reston, James, *151*
Rhee. *See* Syngman Rhee
Rhee, Madam, 71
Ridgway, Lieutenant General Matthew B., 15, 17, 166*n*7; as supreme commander, 18, *103*
Robert, Major General William, 5
Robertson, Colonel W. W., 24
ROK. *See* Republic of Korea
Roman Catholic relief group, 90
Roosevelt, Franklin D.: Japanese-Americans and, 25–26; at Potsdam Conference, 165*n*3
Ross, Lieutenant Bill, 92–95
ROTC. *See* Reserve Officers Training Corps

SA-16, 40–42, *42*, 70, *71*
safe conduct pass leaflets, *101–3*, *107–8*, *130*; fears about, 160–61
SAM. *See* Special Air Missions
Sams, Brigadier General Crawford, 17
Samuels, Bill, 164
Scott, Major, 78, 79, 163–64
secrecy: aircraft for, 72–73; of 581st ARCS Wing, 16–17, 31, 39, 54, 69–70; at Georgetown University, 54; from NSC, 4

Seoul, South Korea: children in, 90; Chinese vases in, 91–92; folk art in, 90; merchants in, 90–91; retaking of, 17; ruins of, *89*, 89–90
Seoul City Air Base, 72
6004th Air Intelligence Service Squadron, 72
South Korea, 5; current status of, 21; friendly fire in, 76–77; map of, *xiv*; reinforcements from, 13, 166*n*6; return from, 163–64. *See also* Fifth Air Force Advance; Seoul, South Korea
Soviet Union, 6, 52; Kasenkina against, 60; post–World War II, 2–3, 165*n*2; VOA and, 59–60. *See also* Stalin, Joseph (premier)
Special Air Missions (SAM), 14
Specialized Warfare Course, 43
spies/special operations agents. *See* black hats
"Spook City," 72
squadron, 33, 42, 166*n*2; helicopter, 72–73, 167*n*7
Stalin, Joseph (premier), 3, 92, *151*; foreign policy of, 2; Mao Tse-tung and, 5, 10–11, 165*n*5; nuclear weapons and, 165*n*2; at Potsdam Conference, 165*nn*2–3; in U.S./UN leaflets, 112–14
Stardust 40, shoot-down of, 19, 21, 63–64, *64*, 73–75
Sung Dynasty, 92
surrender leaflets, *101–3*, *107–8*; fears about, 160–61; from North Korea, *130*
Sustrick, Lieutenant Colonel "Steady Eddy," 69, 71
Syngman Rhee (president), 5, 71; anti-Communism of, 9–10; for reunification, 20–21; safety of, 12–13

Tactical Information
  Department (TID),
  14–15
Tadao, Kano, with Japanese
  general, 91–92
Taiwan, 10, 165*n*3
Taylor, General Maxwell D.,
  20, 78, 166*nn*7–8
TDY. *See* temporary duty
  assignments
temporary duty assignments
  (TDY), 47–48
1300th Air Base Wing, 34
Thompson, James F. (chief,
  Division of Radio
  Operations), 55, 57
TID. *See* Tactical Information
  Department
Tolentino, Pacqing, *66*, 67
Total Power (Walsh), 49
Truman, Harry (president),
  2, 6, 7, 26, 46, 92, 97,
  148; for bombing, 9;
  MacArthur v., 11, 18;
  NSC and, 3, 6; nuclear
  weapons and, 165*n*2;
  United Nations Police
  Action from, 8, 26
Turkey, *116–17*

UN. *See* United Nations
UN General Assembly, 3
Unit 4, pilots of, 13–14
United Nations (UN), 3; on
  attack, 7–8; U.S./UN

leaflets on, *109–10*, *116*,
  117, 162
United Nations Police Action,
  8, 26
United Nations Temporary
  Commission on Korea
  (UNTCOK), 5, 7–8
United States (U.S.), 11–12;
  military buildup in, 5–6;
  military reduction of, 2,
  8; Soviet Union v., 2–3
UN Security Assembly, 7
UN Security Council, 7–8
UNTCOK. *See* United Nations
  Temporary Commission
  on Korea
U.S. *See* United States
U.S. National Security Act, 3
USNS *David C. Shanks*, *62*,
  167*n*3; background of,
  62; duties on, 63

VOA. *See* Voice of America
"Voice" C-47s, 14
Voice of America (VOA),
  2, 11, 43; background
  on, 55–56; Barrett and,
  56–57; education at,
  58–60; funding for,
  56–57; Kohler and, 56,
  58; NSC on, 3; orders to,
  55; Pauker for, 58–59;
  Soviet Union and, 59–60;
  as white hat, 59–60
Voice of UN Command
  (VUNC), 15

volunteers: in ARCS, 43; for
  TDY, 47–48
VUNC. *See* Voice of UN
  Command

Walker, Lieutenant General
  Walton, 12–13, 15
Walsh, Father Edmund A., SJ,
  49–50, 54
war: Cold War, 3–6; First
  World War, 97; germ
  warfare, 18, 19; World
  War II, 24–26, 31, 32, 97
Wasson, Ensign John, 61
weapons: atomic cannon, 93,
  93; British QF twenty-
  five pounder, 99–100;
  field guns, *111*, 155;
  howitzers as, 83, 167*n*3,
  168*n*6; mortars, 94,
  168*n*6; Pershing tank,
  94; personal arms, 91
white hat(s): black hats v.,
  40, 43, 68, 73; leaflets as,
  159; training plan for,
  43; VOA as, 59–60
Wolfgeher, Sergeant Paul A.,
  159, 161
women, 60; Korean, as black
  hats, 71–72; in U.S./UN
  leaflets, *124–27*
World War II: Korean War v.,
  24–26; PW in, 31, 32, 97;
  reactions to, 24–26; U.S.
  invasion and, 25–26